BOUDI(
HER LIFE, TIMES & LEGACY

Further details of Poppyland Publishing titles can be found at
www.poppyland.co.uk
where clicking on the 'Support and Resources' button
will lead to pages specially compiled to support this book

Boudica

Her Life, Times & Legacy

John Davies & Bruce Robinson

POPPYLAND
PUBLISHING

Picture credits
Trustees of the British Museum: page 65 (top)
Steve Bryant: page 6
Colchester Borough Council: page 84
John Davies: pages 22, 23 (top), 24, 30, 31, 34, 49, 55, 56
Mary Davis: page 81
Mike Kwasniak: page 82
Norfolk Museums and Archaeology Service: pages 18, 20, 23 (bottom), 25, 27, 28, 30, 32, 33, 37, 42, 46, 57, 63, 64, 65 (bottom), 70 (bottom), 71 (bottom), 83
Mike Page: page 73
Christopher Pipe/Watermark: pages 29, 40–41
Poppyland Photos: 26, 38, 41, 70–71 (panorama), 79, 85, 88
Andy Pritchett/Uglystudios.com: pages 17, 65 (left)
St Albans Museum: page 68
Bill Seaman: page 86
John Talbot: page 35
Sue White: pages 37, 61

FRONTISPIECE: *Alex Kingston playing the lead role in ITV's 2003 production of* Boudica.
© *ITV/Rex Features*

Contents

Maps

Introduction

A woman for all seasons

There may well have been moments when history and perception turned
their backs on Boudica. Just as sections of public opinion and esteem also
turned on Robert Kett, the Wymondham rebel and ringleader of a Norfolk
peasant uprising during the summer months of 1549, so fame and notoriety
evidently have their down-side. However, four hundred years later Kett was
flavour of the month once more, re-established and even re-invented as a folk
hero who gave his life for a just cause. So with Boudica.

There is no doubt her memory and reputation would have suffered from
mixed reactions at the time of her demise, some time around AD 61. And
no doubt, too, all vestiges and traces of this evidently charismatic and — to
the Romans — troublesome leader were discouraged, removed, destroyed
or swept into the background. This is the prerogative of victors, the way
of conquerors. Therefore, there may also have been a period, even in
East Anglia, when stories and recollections of her exploits were treated as
unwelcome and even dangerous intrusions by those, and their succeeding
generations, who managed to survive the anger of vengeful legions.

First and foremost, ordinary folk of the early Roman period would have
had food, shelter, survival, security and economic stability uppermost in
their minds. Then, as time passed and the trappings of an essentially new

OPPOSITE: *Sculpture of Boudica at Colchester by Jonathan Clarke (1999), distinctly
modern in style.*

Roman way of life slowly began to emerge, and as fresh fashions and ways of doing things began to assert themselves, they might have been tempted to recall her and her exploits as an ancient irrelevance. Even if life was still being lived under the watchful gaze of Roman administrators working for the military occupiers, many would have thought of her rebellion as a blot on the memory, an unwanted reminder of dark and ghastly days when death, fear and ruination stood astride the land.

But public whim and opinion, like fashion, are as malleable as clay. Nowadays, Boudica is back, big time, and has been ever since patriotic Victorians began to search library tomes and records for heroines and examples of queenly bravery, defenders of family and empire who would cast off the yoke of cruel oppressors and carry freedom to the people, and give their all to rightful causes.

Even so, mysteries remain. There is no written record left by Boudica's people, because they did not write. Neither do we have any surviving oral or folk memory. At least, none has been identified. Nor is there a single discovered artefact which she is known to have handled or location at which her past presence is proved beyond doubt. Indeed, there is very little corroboration at all for her existence aside from a few scant sentences by foreign writers who made their records many years after the actual events. And even their words, in their collective entirety, merely shed a pale and possibly distorted light upon a handful of selected events during a few short months of her life.

Perhaps the invaders and the later writers inflated her influence, power and importance purely for propaganda or political purposes. Or for precisely the same reasons, perhaps they attempted to portray her simply as a small player on the margins of the much larger stage of the Roman Empire. The enigma remains. However, it is equally true that we do need our mysteries, our heroes and our heroines. We need to understand that she did exist and that the bare skeleton of the story of the rebellion, as recorded by those later writers, is essentially accurate even if some of the detail may have been spun or presented specially for an ancient audience which needed to know that this pinprick, this inconvenience, was, after some initial difficulty, finally stamped upon and brushed aside.

Vengeance and hope

Thankfully, the one thing we can be certain of is that she did exist. Related evidence of finds from modern archaeological digs, including buried hoards in East Anglia and layers of charred material in Colchester, London and St Albans, all support the story of the rebellion.

But how do we see her now? As a brave woman, certainly. As one who held sway over many of her tribal warriors and some of the neighbouring tribes; who clung to thoughts of vengeance and hope. A woman who fought for her rights. Perhaps we may also view her as one of a long line of female warriors going back to Artemisia who — according to Herodotus — played her full part in campaigns against the Greeks.

Boudica can certainly be seen as a fighter for a cause, a brave and charismatic woman who gave her life for what she thought was right. She can also come across as an all-purpose figurehead, or 'a woman for all seasons'. But in many respects she still remains a ghost, an elusive ideal, a half-glimpsed spectral figure flitting to and fro amongst the shadows and silences of history.

In any event, we evidently still need her, for a current and continually burgeoning interest in the story has spawned a fresh barrage of films, television programmes and books. This is despite the fact that archaeologists have unearthed few new or additional facts about the events of the rebellion of AD 60–61. Indeed, our understanding of the story of the uprising has remained essentially the same for many years. What has changed is an increasing and heightened knowledge of the background, the backdrop against which the great drama was played out. We now have a much fuller understanding of how life was actually lived in Norfolk in the Late Iron Age, what these people did, and in some cases why they did it.

So the purpose and thrust of this book is to position Boudica and her people against the landscape which they and she lived in and knew. This is her Life, Times and Legacy. This, indeed, is the less well known and yet perhaps most enthralling story of all.

Main Tribal Locations in the First Century AD

Life

A watery landscape

To the Greeks and Romans, the people spread across Europe from the Czech Republic to Britain were known as Celts, or Gauls. They are thought to have spoken a cluster of languages and dialects, similar, and possibly related, to those which survive today in the modern Celtic vocabularies of Ireland, Wales, Scotland, Cornwall and Brittany. By the time of Boudica, increasingly settled and well organised societies had been living in Britain for over 3,000 years.

It is not until the second or third decade AD that the Iceni emerge as a single identifiable tribe. Prior to that time there were smaller regional groups of people living across the landscape in tribal factions which fluctuated in size and allegiances over the decades. It was with the minting of coinage inscribed with the letters ECEN that we can see the first real evidence of a united tribe with a clear identity. The Iceni inhabited a land that spread beyond the boundaries of modern Norfolk to encompass north Suffolk and a swathe of fen area within present-day Cambridgeshire. It is not possible to identify the precise boundaries as these would have shifted over time, and probably only stabilised at the time of the Roman conquest.

By the Late Iron Age the weather was marginally warmer and wetter than it is today, and sea levels higher. One effect would have been seen in the region's river systems, where unbanked and unrestrained water courses were generally much larger, wider and more boisterous than at present and, given the periodic effect of tide and storm, more prone to flooding. Most Norfolk rivers run on an approximate east–west west–east axis, making north to south travel more difficult. In this sense it was a difficult landscape, but it was also one put to good use by the adaptable inhabitants. Settlements developed along river valleys and grew and spread over successive generations. The slopes of the river valleys they used for their grazing animals.

There were other notable features of the Late Iron Age landscape in the decades before the Roman invasion. One of the most significant was the vast tidal estuary which then ate into Norfolk's eastern seaboard, covering the area where Great Yarmouth stands today, and which penetrated inland in at least three straggling yet distinct watery strands. One of these, based on the rivers Chet and Yare, ran south of a finger of land – at the head of which was Reedham – and on towards the site of modern Norwich and what subsequently become the location of the Roman regional capital, *Venta Icenorum* (Caistor St Edmund). A second strand meandered in a north-westerly direction on the other side of the Reedham peninsula, ultimately dividing into the rivers Bure and Ant. Yet another finger doubled back on itself towards the sea, thus creating the island of Flegg. Meanwhile, a third strand of the estuary, based on the flow of the River Waveney, helped create yet another tongue of land, now known as Lothingland.

Much later, the Romans were to construct defensive fortifications on either side of the Lothingland estuary, at Caister on Sea (on Flegg island) and Burgh Castle (Lothingland), while their barges and boats ranged inland as far as *Venta Icenorum* and Brampton, which became the centre of a pottery-making industry.

People in view

Iron Age people clearly exploited this vast region of waterways and river systems, including the Bure, the Yare and the Waveney, although nothing in the way of evidence for waterborne commerce or fishing activity has actually come to light. The remains of one log boat, believed to be part of a five-metre (16-foot) rowing boat, was unearthed by a dredger at Smallburgh in 1927. Although this spectacular find showed the potential for archaeological preservation, it was subsequently dated to the Anglo Saxon period. Today, these vast inland waterways are much more restricted, but Breydon Water, next to Great Yarmouth, is a surviving relic of the old estuary.

More centrally within Norfolk, tracts of thick woodland stretched across the heavy boulder clay region in a vaguely triangular shape, from East Dereham in the north to Attleborough and Diss in the south. Two surviving remnants of what was then largely virgin forest are Wayland Wood, near Watton, and Foxley Wood, near Bawdeswell. The area north-east of Norwich was also wooded and probably remained so until after the Iron Age. However, it would be a mistake to see this wildwood as an impenetrable barrier to communities and travellers. By the Late Iron Age settlement sites and lines of communication had already made significant inroads right across the area.

Environmental factors also played a part in shaping the landscape, for in the north-west of the county, roughly around Docking, the quality of the soil had already deteriorated. The high chalk areas had been cleared during the Neolithic and Bronze Ages, having been over-exploited and over-farmed for generations. This led to a thinness of the soil, particularly on the upper slopes, and by the Late Iron Age even this was being washed away. Arable activity, aside from pockets of pasture, was declining or had even stopped altogether. This battle to maintain soil quality and fertility goes on today.

In the west of the area a quite different sort of coastline — now largely concealed by modern agricultural and forestry activities — stretched from Wisbech to Downham Market. This distinctive region, now known as fenland, must have been a forbidding area for ordinary folk for it demanded, and supported, a completely different way of life. It is likely that the inhabitants were different in character, too, wresting a hard living from creek and reed, fish, eel and fowl, rather than from the land. If today's situation is anything to go by, then they may have spoken a different dialect, too.

Wind and water

The overall shape of Norfolk has altered considerably since the Late Iron Age. We know that the north coast lay some distance beyond its current

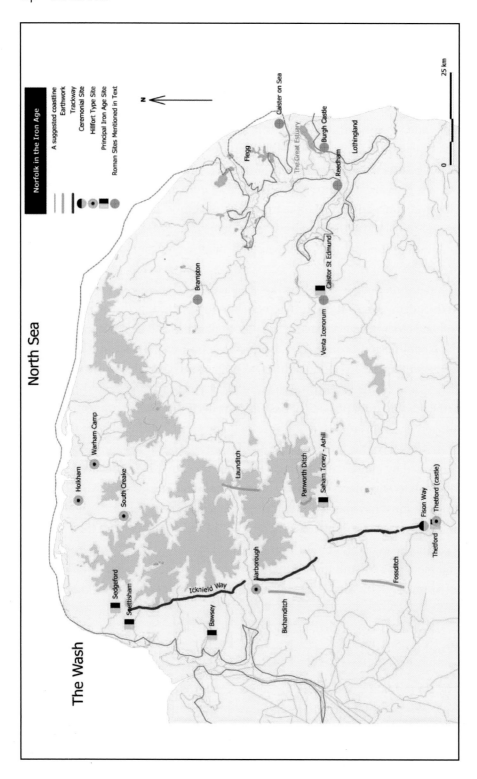

position. For example, research surrounding the discovery of the so-called Seahenge timbered monument on the present beach at Holme next the Sea — which actually dates from the earlier Bronze Age period — shows that this site originally stood in an area of marginal shoreland between dry land and the sea. This indicates how far further north the coastline extended some 2,000 years before Boudica's birth. Even during the Roman period the Norfolk coast still extended several kilometres north of its present position.

A changing coastline has also been reported in the east. The silting-up of the great estuary in the area of modern Great Yarmouth first occurred during the late Roman years. Today, once again, the sea has also started to reclaim land along the east coast. Lost settlements long since covered by the sea have been recorded at Eccles and elsewhere, including Dunwich in Suffolk.

A glance at the map of their territory reveals why the Iceni enjoyed a degree of geographical isolation within Britain. To the west, the Wash and the huge tract of watery fen must have provided a barrier between them and the Corieltauvi of Lincolnshire. At that time the fenland was undrained and the open sea reached much further inland than it does today. Admittedly, there was an easier land route towards the south connecting the Iceni with their southern neighbours, the Trinovantes, but even so, travel into and out of the Icenian area by land can never have been entirely straightforward.

Given the difficulties involved in travelling overland to other parts of Britain, the opportunities provided by water transport must have seemed far more attractive. The Iceni would have had active seaborne contacts with other areas, for over a hundred miles of coastline and innumerable rivers and estuaries were under their control. This means of transport and communication would have been of fundamental importance and, indeed, a part of the Icenian character. Maritime and river usage was undoubtedly a distinctive feature of the region. Travel around the eastern seaboard of Britain by sea would have been much quicker than by land, and would have connected this area to a much wider network of peoples.

For the Iceni, contacts with those on the far side of the English Channel and North Sea would have been easier and possibly more regular than with people in the far west and north of Britain, and as trading opportunities developed — associated with agriculture, for example — so they would have been made easier by using water transport.

Working in the landscape

In the Late Iron Age the Norfolk landscape was a patchwork of small fields, ditches, hedges and tracks, farms and settlements, stockyards and droveways. We are now also increasingly aware of the existence of important ritual areas and sites. Many settlements were situated close to rivers and, as time progressed, they developed and grew in a linear fashion along the valley bottoms. Fields were cultivated through the use of wooden ploughs pulled by teams of oxen. In poorer soil areas, such as the chalk uplands and in what is now Breckland, in south Norfolk, sheep and cattle predominated. Pigs rummaged in the central wildwood areas and winter grain was stored in cylindrical pits covered by lids of plaited basket weave smeared with clay. This was a very clever system. The damp sides of the pits actually reacted with the outer layers of grain to create carbon dioxide, which in turn prevented the remainder of the grain from germinating. Meanwhile, a good proportion of stock was over-wintered on hay, grain and fair-weather grazing, while any surplus was killed and the meat smoked, salted or dried. Smoke would have wafted from any number of smithies and kilns.

Iron had been in general use in Europe for some 300 years before a knowledge of smithing techniques reached Norfolk in about 700 BC. Bronze continued to be used for decorative metalwork throughout the Iron Age, but iron was important for more functional items. Very slowly, iron became the predominant material, largely because it produced the most efficient cutting edge. Some low grade ores were available in the area. The Greensand deposits of west Norfolk were the most important. Over the years the smiths became skilled specialist craftsmen making weapons such as swords and spear heads, horse harness, and agricultural implements such as knives, billhooks, sickles and spade tips. Even so, and somewhat surprisingly, the use of flint tools still lingered beside that of metal in Norfolk and other parts of East Anglia throughout the Iron Age.

Formal towns did not exist in the Iron Age. They were a Roman introduction to Britain. However, some large settlement concentrations appeared in southern areas in the decades before Boudica's birth. They generally go under the name of *oppida*, and they have only recently been identified in Norfolk. One such large settlement has been found at Caistor

Ploughing fields beside a settlement in Iron Age Norfolk

St Edmund, and another at Thetford, where it guarded the river fords on the Icknield Way. The best example identified so far, however, is in and around Saham Toney in central west Norfolk. A ritually filled shaft was also discovered there many years ago, adjacent to the settlement which sprawled over several kilometres.

By and large, however, and aside from the *oppida*, Iceni settlements seem to have been small farmsteads. They grew early types of wheat (emmer and spelt) and barley, a good proportion of which was used for brewing. This latter activity must have been very time-consuming, so it was clearly an important ingredient in their lives and may even have provided the main and perhaps safest drink. The alternative was rainwater or water from streams and rivers which were occasionally vulnerable to pollution from decaying vegetation and animal carcases.

The general body of evidence for Iceni settlements is slender, however. One of the problems of Late Iron Age archaeology is finding identifiable traces of occupation. Iron itself tends to survive very poorly, and wood and wattle rot and degrade. There is also the added problem that because of a

An Iron Age farmstead in Norfolk: illustration by Ivan Lapper.

lack of dating evidence it is difficult to be certain that some rural settlements actually belong to the Iron Age. Their use of friable pottery, metal corrosion, and centuries of farming activity have also contributed to a lack of dating evidence in the ground. Consequently, it can be very difficult to distinguish between farms of the Bronze Age, the Iron Age or even the Roman period.

Some sites, particularly on the edge of the Norfolk fens, were still only seasonally occupied at this time. Many of the settlements that Boudica and her family would have known were merely the size of modern farmyards. In general, they tended to comprise two or three circular houses made of mud and timber walls with thatched roofs which were warmed by a central fire. In many cases, new homes were simply built over the top of older ones.

The burial mystery

Not only do we have very little evidence for the settlements, but we have even less for what happened to people after they died. Evidence for the burial of Iron Age people is rare across Britain. Most of the very few examples of Iron Age human remains from Norfolk are incomplete skeletons, and these pieces of skull, shoulder, leg or arm might actually be the remains of ritual practices rather than burials, as was the case with animal bones and other domestic objects on Iron Age sites. A small number of cremations have been found, but full cremation cemeteries are unknown in the land of the Iceni.

This lack of burials is even more strange when it is considered that the Iceni were thought to be a war-like society. And yet not even the massacres associated with Boudica's battles have left us with cemeteries of dead people. So, what were they doing with their dead?

Whatever they did, it was a process that has left almost no trace today. Even the burning of bodies leaves evidence in the form of burnt bone. The answer may be that when people died their bodies were left outside, perhaps on wooden platforms and exposed to the elements. The bodies would then have decayed and their remains been carried off by wild animals or dispersed — perhaps into Norfolk's many waterways. Despite this suggestion, the almost complete lack of evidence for the dead remains a real puzzle. If people's bodies were all left outside, then the scale of the practice must have meant that decaying bodies were a regular feature in the landscape.

People today are invariably concerned or disappointed that we have not discovered the site of Boudica's final resting place. However, this is not surprising in the context of the normal situation of the time. What is perhaps more surprising is the lack of bodies associated with the fighting and the massacres which did take place during Boudica's reign, which must have resulted in very large numbers of dead.

The wider world

To Roman soldiers about to board cross-Channel ships, Britain must have seemed a cold, damp, disconcertingly mysterious and even backward place at the outer edge of the Empire. To them, it was something akin to a Rhineland 'border' territory where the tribes were unruly and designed towns were unknown. However, British Iron Age society was highly developed in ways that the Romans would not have appreciated. Even today, the depth and richness of this culture is still not fully understood. Boudica's people could not explain their society to us because they did not have writing, so their thoughts, deeds and beliefs were never documented. Instead, elements of their culture were passed down through oral tradition in stories and songs and these, of course, ultimately merged with folklore and legend.

Iceni society was elaborately structured. The people lived in harmony with their environment, and almost all men and women spent their lives on the land, raising crops and managing woodland. They were also a deeply religious people with their own highly sophisticated belief system. They nurtured and revered the highly skilled metal workers; indeed, craftsmen enjoyed a high status in society. People built their houses cleverly, too, using local materials and methods designed to cope admirably with the vagaries of the British climate. Mysterious as it may have seemed to Roman troops more used to Mediterranean warmth and ways, this was still a mature and vibrant society, and although it was very different it was just as successful as the Roman model.

A beautifully crafted terret ring, part of a horse harness, made by an Iceni craftsman.

The Mediterranean world certainly knew about Britain. Throughout the Neolithic and Bronze Age periods trading networks had slowly developed; tin, for example, had been shipped from the West Country for centuries. Herodotus, writing circa 420 BC, knew that his Mediterranean world acquired supplies from the 'Tin Islands', even though he was unsure where they were. In about 330 BC Pytheas the Greek may have actually visited Britain and seen the tin mines before sailing into Arctic waters and subsequently returning home.

Whether in the two centuries before the Boudican revolt people in Britain actually knew anything of the destruction of Carthage, the Petra stone carvings in Jordan, Antony and Cleopatra, or even the revolt of Spartacus, is also not clear. But they certainly knew about mainland Europe and about the commercial power-base of the Mediterranean coastal ports, and they would have watched with interest and alarm the swelling military and political strength of that distant Empire with its capital in Rome. More to the point, it is quite likely that some Iceni warriors had already fought against the legions of Caesar in Gaul.

So Britain in the Late Iron Age was by no means isolated in a political and economic sense, even though, geographically, it must still have seemed distant and mysterious to the citizens of Rome, for whom it lay at the mysterious outer edge of their otherwise familiar world.

Society and tribal centres

The first mention of the tribal name emanates from Caesar's British campaign of 54 BC. He names the *Cenimagni* as one of five tribes which sent deputations to him. The difference in the name may mean that this was a smaller faction or sub-group of the people who lived in the region. It is not until some fifty years later that we can detect a coming together of these smaller groups with the appearance, across the whole area, of coinage bearing the word ECEN. The next historical mention of the name was made by Tacitus. He wrote that in AD 47 the Iceni paid tribute (tax) to Rome, as well as supplying the Empire with a quota of auxiliary troops.

The chief, or king, was at the apex of tribal society in much of Late Iron Age Britain, although it is quite possible there were different social structures in different parts of the country at the same time. A parallel can be seen in later North America where Indian tribes, although living side by side, were organised very differently depending on their geographical location, the natural resources available to them, and the sort of contacts they had with other peoples.

An Iron Age chieftain's power embraced a complex combination of political, religious and military roles. They were the leaders of the tribe's warriors, who were bound by loyalty, and they were supported by a priestly class called Druids. Most people, though, were simple farmers who spent their days working the land.

So far it has not proved possible to indicate that a single specific site in Norfolk was the location of the royal household of the Iceni, although archaeology has given us some candidates. Caistor St Edmund was one such important settlement. The evidently prosperous settlement at Saham

Toney must be another attractive candidate. A further possibility is that the Iceni might have had a 'mobile' royal court which moved from one place to another. The concept is not entirely unknown. Twelve hundred years later King John was hardly ever still. In his case, the source of political, military and legal power was sited wherever he and his officials happened to be on a particular day.

Kingdom of the horse

The Celts were renowned for their prowess in horsemanship. The horse seems to have had a very special place within some Late Iron Age societies, and it is the one recurring motif on Iron Age coinage. It was also used in other ways. In about 200 BC, when the Atrebates tribe of central southern England decided to display a giant image on a prominent chalk hillside, they also chose the image of a horse. Horses were certainly very important to the Iceni — apparently more so than to some other tribes. A majority of their objects found by archaeologists today are horse-related items, and the Iceni territory may truly be described as 'the Kingdom of the Horse'.

Within Iceni territory, horses would have been used for pulling chariots. The use of chariots had continued in Britain after they had become obsolete in Gaul at the time of Julius Caesar's campaigns, and Caesar described how the Britons used them in warfare. Some tribes in northern Britain continued to use chariots into the late first century AD. Chariot fittings have been found

A pair of linch pins from Attleborough. Length 47mm and 49mm.

The decorated heads of two linch pins from Attleborough, showing the triplet symbol on their ends. Diameters 28mm and 29mm

widely in Britain, but soil conditions have not preserved the actual wooden vehicles.

In Norfolk, over one hundred items of Late Iron Age horse equipment have been found, including terrets (rings to hold traces), bridle bits, linch-pins, strap unions, horn-caps, hooks and harness mounts. This total is far higher than for any other English county. Four Norfolk metalwork hoards (one at Ringstead, two at Saham Toney, one at nearby Ovington) were also dominated by horse equipment. The importance of horses to the Iceni can be appreciated by the fact that similar items are completely absent from other larger parts of southern England.

There have been some particularly impressive discoveries of horse harness equipment in Norfolk. At Saham Toney a group of items found in 1992 included harness fittings, rings, worn horse bits and enamelled horse decorations, all of a type and design popular during the first century AD.

Iron Age bridle bit from Swanton Morley. External diameter of each ring is 75mm.

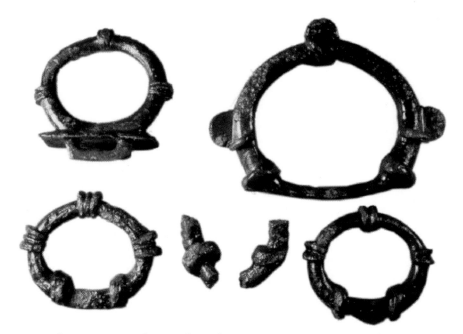

A group of Iron Age terrets discovered at Saham Toney in 1992. Maximum diameter of top right terret 115mm.

As mentioned earlier, Saham Toney is thought to have been a settlement of significant size and importance at the time of Boudica. In 2000, an elaborate enamelled bridle bit also found at Swanton Morley may have been owned by a high-status person. At King's Lynn, a set of copper alloy objects was found, including two enamelled flat-ring terrets and another flat-ring terret, all of a native design.

Horses were clearly central to the culture of the Iceni, and considerable wealth was expended on chariot harness fittings of great beauty. Horses and their highly decorated horse equipment duly became an elaborate symbol of Icenian identity.

Discovery at Snettisham

In 1948, in a field at Ken Hill near Snettisham, a tractor driver found what he thought were pieces of wire or old metal snagged around his plough. He had in fact made the first discovery on this site of a form of Late Iron Age jewellery which we know as 'torcs'. Ken Hill is a raised piece of land not far from the sea shore, overlooking the Wash. The view to the west carries into Lincolnshire, while a vast swathe of north-west Norfolk can be surveyed inland. Two years after the first discovery, another agricultural worker had a similar experience.

By this time it was realised that this site was very special indeed, and it was slowly being associated with a growing collection of Iron Age torcs. Exciting additional hoards were subsequently excavated at the same location in 1964, 1968, 1973, 1989 and 1990. So far, in total, some 180 torcs have been recovered from eleven hoards at Ken Hill.

Torcs are a form of ring designed to be worn around the neck. The name reflects the fact that some examples were made of twisted strands of metal. However, there are different forms of torc, and not all of them were manufactured in this way. They were sometimes made of gold, sometimes silver, sometimes electrum (an alloy of the two) and sometimes of plain bronze. The majority of torcs from the whole of Britain come from East Anglia, and most of those are from Ken Hill. The locations of almost all the torcs recovered in Norfolk so far, at Snettisham, Bawsey, North Creake,

The complete Snettisham Treasure, before the 1990 British Museum excavation

Several seasons of excavation at Sedgeford have proved fruitful in understanding the story of a village which has existed on the same site from the time of the Iceni to the present day.

Sedgeford, Marham, Narford and East Winch, are in the west and north-west of the county.

In 2003 another magnificent electrum torc was found in south Norfolk and declared legally Treasure. This torc is very special for two reasons. First, it is the only precious metal example to have been discovered away from west Norfolk, and second, it is an exceptionally beautiful example and has survived complete. Details of its workmanship show strong similarities to some of the Snettisham examples, and it is likely to have originated from the same workshop. It is fascinating to imagine what important person might have carried this most valuable item, which was clearly an object of high status, away from the north-west during the early or middle years of the first century BC.

Where did the metal come from to make the torcs? The answer is that other objects made from precious metals were imported from the Continent and then melted down by the Iceni craftsmen in order to manufacture their own items. This practice is also evidence that significant trade links existed with continental Europe at that time.

Torcs of the town

Torcs are known from continental Europe from the fifth century BC through to the first century AD. On the Continent, buried torcs have long been regarded as votive offerings. The Snettisham hoards all seem to date from the early first century BC. Torcs were also the classic, sought-after status symbol of Iron Age society. Sculptures depict Celtic warriors wearing them, historians describe them as an essential part of Celtic battle array, and Boudica herself is said to have worn one. A torc might be seen as the equivalent of a royal crown as worn by a king or queen today. They may also have been seen as items worn to express tribal identity, or an association with the area. Many were thick and heavy, so how were they worn?

Although most torcs could be twisted open and then worn around the neck, they would have been too heavy to wear for any length of time. Some, therefore, may have been used only during specific ceremonies. Other lighter and less flexible torcs may have been continually worn, much as finger rings are worn today. A group of large but hollow or tubular gold torcs was discovered at Snettisham. These were clearly designed to be worn for relatively short periods.

Terminal of torc found in south-west Norfolk in 2003

They are very light to hold but are also very fragile, though they would have looked spectacular when worn in tribal functions and gatherings.

Excavations by the British Museum showed that the Snettisham torcs were deposited in 'nests' very carefully cut into the ground. The items within each individual nest had also been separated internally according to metal type (gold, silver, alloy) and also by colour. The most valuable pieces in

A gold tubular torc from Snettisham, Hoard A. Diameter 190mm.

some hoards were also separated from each other by layers of earth. This elaborately structured process appears to reinforce the interpretation of Snettisham, like its continental counterparts, as a ritual deposit.

Structured deposition has been identified in relation to many other aspects of Iron Age life. The carefully ordered hoarding seen at the torc findspots points to a significant location within a landscape evidently littered with special places and sanctuaries. Domestic occupation seems to have been interspersed with a series of shrines and sacred places. Indeed, this corner of north-west Norfolk may have been a focus of Iron Age wealth, importance and political authority at the time. Not only were torcs concentrated there, but most of the gold coins discovered in Norfolk were also buried within the same geographical region.

The rich north-west was separated from the rest of Norfolk by a row of earthwork enclosures constructed at intervals in a north to south line. They were located at strategic positions on the boundary between the better free-draining soils to the west and the heavier, more difficult, soils to the east, and they were constructed at Holkham, Warham, South Creake, Narborough and Thetford, with another possible example at Bawsey. They seem to stand like sentry-boxes, or markers, at the edge of a territory and over the approaches of the Icknield Way.

The impressive Iron Age earthwork known as Warham Camp commands a view of the surrounding country-side; when it was built, the ditch between the two ramparts was two metres deeper than it is today. The inner rampart was once topped with a wooden palisade.

Home-made coins

The large number of coins that have been turning up through metal-detection in Norfolk in recent years suggest that coin use among the Iceni was much more widespread than had previously been thought. The first coinage to be used in Britain had been produced on the Continent, in what is now northern France, during the early second century BC. Gold staters from the period of Caesar's Gallic War have been found at many locations in Norfolk, almost exclusively in hoards.

Coinage was first produced by the Iceni during the second quarter of the first century BC. One of the first types used carries the head of Apollo on the obverse, coupled with a leggy wolf with snapping jaws on the reverse. We now

Norfolk Wolf type gold coins. Diameter 17mm.

know that the first silver types, known as Early Face Horse, were in use at the same time as Norfolk Wolf staters. In fact, we can also say that Iceni coinage contained different denominations as well as both gold and silver types. There were gold staters and gold quarter staters. Small silver minims are still rare finds today, but they were used alongside larger silver units within a full monetary system.

The gradual coming together of the smaller tribal sub-groups is reflected in the increasingly uniform appearance of the coinage, which culminated in the more standardised Pattern-Horse types. In the early decades AD, some Icenian coins were inscribed with letters, which may have been the names of tribal rulers. ANTED may have been the name of such a leader. This person was followed by ECEN and ECE, whose names echo that of the tribe. Indeed,

*Pattern-horse
type silver coin.
Diameter 13mm.*

the eventual tribal unity is expressed with the appearance of the coinage
marked ECEN.

Evidence for coin production has been found within the Iceni area in the
form of clay moulds, pellets made from silver being prepared in these moulds
before being struck as finished coins. Coin moulds have been found at
Saham Toney and Thetford and also at Needham, three sites in central and
southern Norfolk. It seems likely that the Iceni ceased producing their own
coinage after the first tribal revolt in AD 47.

Hoards and deposits

Many hoards were buried within Norfolk during the Late Iron Age. These
include coin hoards as well as deposits containing other forms of metalwork
such as drinking vessels. Some of these were located at special places in the
landscape and can be considered ritual deposits. These forms of hoard were
not buried in containers but were very carefully positioned in the ground.
Other hoards were buried in more of a hurry, presumably during times of
stress, and these were more commonly placed in pottery containers.

A number of hoards containing gold coins were buried during the mid-
first century BC, and they may relate to Caesar's expeditions to Britain. In
Norfolk, they are found around the north and north-west coast.

Some later coin and metalwork deposits throw light on events during
the Boudican uprising itself. Metalwork hoards found in both Norfolk and
Suffolk were buried at the time of the revolt. In contrast to gold coins buried
in north-west Norfolk in the previous century, they are concentrated in south
and east Norfolk, and north Suffolk, and three main groups can be identified.

The first group of hoards is centred around Thetford and extends east along
the Waveney valley. A second group is centred on Caistor St Edmund, further
to the north. And there is a third group, which lay beyond the modern county
boundary, in north-east Cambridgeshire. That area, between March, Stonea
and Chatteris, was also part of Icenian territory.

It is attractive to imagine that one of these areas, or possibly all of
them, were the storm centres where the initial Boudican uprising ignited.
If so, this underlines a growing impression that Breckland and its
surrounding countryside might have been closely involved in the events of
AD 60–61.

Another metalwork hoard from Hockwold, on the southern fen edge,
comprises items which were entirely of Roman manufacture and includes
parts of at least seven silver wine cups. They had been hammered flat
and were clearly a smith's bullion. At Brandon, on the other hand,
three vessels were found hidden beneath a large bronze cauldron which
had been buried upside down to provide cover. One of the saucepans
originated from Gaul.

In 1982 a site at
Crownthorpe, south of
Norwich, yielded a set of
drinking vessels which
exhibited a fusion of
Roman and native

A hoard of Icenian
silver coins, buried at
Honingham at the time of the
revolt.

The Crownthorpe hoard of drinking vessels

tastes and styles. A large straining vessel was initially revealed, into which another group of vessels had been crushed. These included a unique and charming pair of Roman-style drinking cups which had been decorated with Celtic-style ducks on their handles. This form of drinking set would have been commonly used within a Roman household. It was probably owned by a local prominent Icenian person who had been hoping to enhance his status by adopting some of the Roman ways of doing things. It clearly backfired on him, because the Crownthorpe hoard dates from the period of the Boudican rebellion in AD 60. It had been deliberately hidden in some haste. Could its owner have been fleeing from Boudica's rebels who were intent on revenge against the Romans and their friends?

A distinct identity

There are no contemporary accounts that tell us what the Iceni looked like. Other elements of their material culture suggest that these people projected a distinct identity, and it is very likely that this would have been expressed in the way they dressed, particularly for special occasions such as feasts, ceremonies and going into battle. It is the coin evidence, once again, which provides a partial answer.

Bury A type silver coin. Actual diameter 15mm.

A number of early Icenian silver coin types show contemporary representations of people's faces. Types such as the Early Face-Horse series depict individuals and probably represent those of high status, including Icenian chieftains or religious leaders. The Bury A coin type shows a clean-shaven face wearing a head-dress with a prominent head-band. The Bury B series shows an individual wearing another form of head-dress, with a head-band decorated with a line of X-shaped decorations. The head-dress itself shows twisted rope-like spirals, twisting backwards, and with an elaborate spiral of a horn-shaped attachment covering the ear. The whole effect resembles a North American Indian feathered head-dress. Could this be an early form of dreadlocks?

The Saham Toney type appears to show a bearded — but not moustached

— individual. The head is covered with 'pellets', which again may depict an elaborate form of head-dress. On the other hand, they may represent a very full head of curly hair.

Meet the Druids

The Druids played a central role in Iron Age society by acting as intermediaries between the people and their gods. However, their role was much broader than that of simply presiding over religious ceremonies. They were teachers,

The Saham Toney coin type gives a hint of what the Iceni looked like. Diameter 14mm.

astronomers, the keepers of tribal record and memory, and also the arbiters of justice. But having enjoyed unparalleled levels of influence, their role was then seriously curtailed by the Roman invasion. In reply, they retreated into remote parts of Wales and Anglesey and slowly began to act as a unifying force of resistance to the invaders.

Caesar described a Druids' gathering where 'a great number of young men gather about them for the sake of instruction and hold them in great honour. It is they who decide in almost all disputes, public and private.' Pliny the Elder wrote of their religious role, describing the symbolic importance they attached to mistletoe, oak trees and oak groves. He also mentioned that they practised a sort of moon worship, involving binding the horns of bulls, wearing white cloaks and also animal sacrifice. He evidently viewed Druidism as a sort of British magic.

The main problem in trying to fit the Druids into the archaeology of the period is that they are, by and large, undetectable. They have left no real archaeological evidence. Oak groves and priestly robes disappear and leave no trace, and Druidic images are unknown in Britain, or at least remain unrecognised. Nevertheless, it would be reasonable to suggest that Druids were active within the territory of the Iceni. It is very likely they held great sway in the earlier years, particularly before the Iceni became a united single group, but their influence would have been removed from the region when, or even before, the Romans created the Icenian client kingdom.

Meet the gods

Immediately prior to the revolt against the Romans — according to Roman sources — the Iceni queen and her followers called for guidance and support from the goddess Andraste. The writer Dio specifically mentions the 'grave of Andate' as the place where they conducted their rites.

In fact archaeology now shows that the people of the Late Iron Age had a very different conception of religion to us and to the Romans. Their everyday life was embedded with actions that made reference to spiritual beliefs and to their gods. Unfortunately, there is a lack of direct information from the native population about their religion, because they have left no written accounts, and many modern descriptions of Celtic religion base their interpretation on the later situation during the Roman period, which was probably quite different from that of the pre-Conquest years.

Generally, there were two types of locations where religious activities were carried out during the Late Iron Age in Britain. There were shrines, which had at least an element of man-made construction, and there were special places in the landscape. These were completely natural locations and could be watery locations, such as a river or spring, or perhaps a grove of trees. Precious metalwork offerings left by Iron Age people are often found at such sites.

A religious site of regional importance was excavated at Fison Way (Gallows Hill) at Thetford. The grand and unusual nature of the site led to an initial suggestion that this rectangular timber enclosure might have been Boudica's palace. However, we no longer believe that idea, and a religious function now seems unmistakable. A site was first constructed there during the Middle Iron Age, and by the time of the Roman conquest this had become a double-ditched enclosure. Shortly after that it was enlarged, and concentric rows of close timber fencing were constructed, which may have served as an artificial oak grove. It is very likely that Boudica visited the site to take part in religious rituals, even if it did not serve as her residence.

Reconstruction by Sue White of the enclosure at Fison Way, Thetford, Phase III.

In conquered provinces such as Britain the Romans often imposed Roman names on native deities in order to subtly convert local religions to their own. This may be seen as a form of cultural arrogance, forcibly converting native populations to the religion of their conquerors. The process was probably resisted by the local population, and it would certainly have been an additional cause of friction with the Romans during the years leading up to the revolts of AD 47 and AD 60.

A reverential life

Among Iron Age societies at large there was an awareness of 'other worlds', of marginal lands and places, and perhaps of an underworld. Iron Age people often chose water-edge sites for the careful deposition of metalwork objects chosen as religious offerings. Such metalwork objects, including swords and shields, were often ritually 'broken' before being deposited. The chosen locations where these offerings were made were considered to be very special places in the landscape.

Watery sites and locations defined as boundaries were important for this purpose. There was, for example, a special reverence for places where land, sky and water met together. Some years ago at Ashill, adjacent to the Iron Age settlement of Saham Toney, evidence was found for a deep well which contained a mass of archaeological evidence. This was discovered to be a specially dug ritual shaft which had been deliberately and carefully filled at, possibly, annual intervals with layers of pottery fragments, hazel twigs, and other items. This layering effect has a clear parallel with the Snettisham site at Ken Hill where the torcs had been carefully deposited in layers within the hoard pits.

Iron Age people were also very aware of the changing seasons and of the natural rhythms of nature. Most round houses, for example, seem to have

Experimental archaeology, such as that undertaken at Butser in Hampshire, can help us develop ideas of how the people of the Iron Age may have lived.

had entrances facing south-east towards the rising sun. There may have been practical reasons for this, such as achieving additional warmth or even airing bedding to get rid of fleas. However, it does seem that tradition and belief dictated and dominated their way of life. In other words, belief and ritual were an integral part of everyday life.

When the Romans arrived, therefore, they found a diverse mix of tribal societies and a landscape where religion and daily life were closely integrated. In the face of this intricate and complex civilisation, the Romans attempted to impose a new way of doing things based on their own Mediterranean model. What the conquerors could never appreciate was the depth and resilience of the native culture. After the Romans left, and despite four hundred years of occupation, many aspects of this indigenous culture rose to the surface once again and lived on.

The Iceni code

Archaeology is also showing how Iron Age societies living across Britain were quite different from one another. The Iceni, for example, did things in their own particular way. They had their own very strong identity which they expressed through the way they dressed, the design of the things they made, and their behaviour. They were deeply religious and adhered to strict religious rituals and behaviour. Thus life among the Iceni was carefully structured. All these aspects of their behaviour are reflected in their material objects, which we find through archaeology and in the way they have been deposited in the ground.

Very little of what the Iron Age people left behind was accidentally dropped. Most of it was intentionally placed in the ground, or in water. We have already mentioned the way that precious torcs were carefully placed in structured hoards in the ground at Snettisham. When animal bones such as cattle skulls, and pieces of human skeletons and skulls are found, these also appear to have been often carefully buried at significant places on settlements or within the wider landscape. We know they were doing things in a planned and careful way. But what was the real significance of this behaviour?

The Iceni did not have writing. This form of communication was not introduced until the Roman period. Everything was spoken and passed down by way of an elaborate oral tradition. Through this ritualized and structured social behaviour Boudica's people have left us with a complex 'code' to decipher, in their symbols, settlement layouts, and in the way they deposited their possessions in the ground. The closer we look at the 'code', the more complex it becomes. It is mysterious to us now, but what further riches of knowledge await?

The shift south

Until the early first century BC the north-west of Norfolk and the area around Snettisham was the dominant focus of wealth, status and power within the Icenian region. This was to change dramatically, for by the mid-first century BC the north-west's power and influence were waning. The population was growing steadily and beginning to spread right across the region. This shift, and the new external contacts with traders and people across the sea, caused an emphatic shift in political power.

It was this increasing population pressure on the landscape that caused pioneers, followed by settlers, to move right across Icenian territory and even into some of the poorer areas of marginal land to live. Thus the claylands of central Norfolk saw the arrival of farmers who, for the first time, were able to break up the heavier soils with a new form of iron-tipped plough, called the ard. It was also at this stage that larger settlements in the south began to develop.

In central Norfolk, Saham Toney grew up at the junction of the river Wissey and the Watton Brook on the boundary between the light Breck-edge soils and heavier clays. Evidence for Iron Age settlement of regional importance is suggested by the extent and nature of the finds being discovered today.

In south Norfolk a major Late Iron Age settlement grew up close to the confluence of the rivers Tas and Yare at Caistor St Edmund. This was eventually developed into the Roman *civitas capital* of *Venta Icenorum*. A

Landscape near Saham Toney: agricultural land today, as it was in the time of the Iceni, who were able to bring the soil here under cultivation with their iron-tipped ploughs. Any impression that this was a backwater, however, is quite wrong: in the Late Iron Age this area formed an important settlement which has provided significant finds for archaeologists.

third major settlement developed across the Thetford area at a strategic location which dominated both land and river routes. The Icknield Way crossed the rivers Thet and Little Ouse, adjacent to the site of another major enclosure of hillfort type. The major religious complex at Fison Way was integral to the status of the settlement.

An enamelled harness mount from Fison Way, Thetford. Diameter 73mm.

The area of south Norfolk became increasingly prominent and eventually replaced Snettisham as the major tribal focus during the later first century BC. By the eve of the Roman conquest it was the two Breckland sites in the west and Caistor in the east that had become the main political *foci* of the Iceni.

First contact

Some time in 55 BC some ninety-eight strange and powerful transport vessels, together with a number of warships, were spotted off the southern shores of Britain. They were there at the behest of Julius Caesar who had been engaged in a bitterly fought campaign to subjugate Gaul. It was during this campaign that he conceived the idea of invading the mysterious islands just off the edge of the known Roman world.

Caesar may have had a number of issues uppermost in mind. An extension of his war to Britain could be explained as being for the security of Gaul. After all, the country had been acting as a refuge for dissident Gauls, while for decades British warriors, many acting as mercenaries, had been crossing to Gaul to fight against his legions. Thus Caesar decided on an initial scouting and intelligence gathering expedition, as well as a show of force, in 55 BC.

Prior to the expedition a number of British tribes had sent envoys to Caesar to offer their submission. He accepted, and sent the envoys back with a Gaul named Commius. Commius had been installed as a puppet king of the Gallic Atrebates who lived in the territories north of the Seine. He was already well known in Britain, and was expected to carry out a sort of 'hearts and minds' campaign there and to drum up support for Rome.

In the event things did not go smoothly for Caesar. The troops made a difficult coastal landing near Deal, in Kent, only to meet stiff resistance. Then many of his vessels were severely damaged shortly afterwards by an unexpectedly high tide and by storms. In addition, winter was fast approaching. This initial contact was not an unqualified success for the great general, although it did allow him to return some impressive dispatches to

Roman soldiers prepare for battle; illustration by Jamel Akib.

the Roman Senate. However, it was clear that this initial contact needed to be followed by a longer and more decisive campaign. Caesar repaired his ships and returned to Gaul.

The return of Caesar

The fact that foreign vessels loaded with troops had visited the shores of England, however briefly, would have sparked considerable concern among those living in the south. The ruthless ability and efficiency of the Roman legions was well known, even among the British. Mercenaries returning from foreign wars would certainly have talked about them, and by the Late Iron Age the upper echelons of some southern British communities would have been perfectly aware of the military events unfolding in Gaul.

Meanwhile, Caesar bided his time. Back in Gaul he revised his plans, bolstered his fleet to an estimated 800 ships, and ordered five legions and 2,000 cavalry to stand by. The next year, 54 BC, he set sail again, and this time failure was not an option. In spite of strong opposition a significant bridgehead was established on the Kent coast. Early skirmishes and sniping exchanges with the local opposition were ultimately successful, and then, when everything was in place, Caesar marched towards the river Thames and the small community and crossing place which subsequently grew and became known as London. This time his objectives seem to have been fully met.

The legions crossed the Thames and duly confronted and overcame stiff resistance from Cassivellaunus, king of the Catuvellauni, one of the first British leaders to emerge out of the mists of history. His links with resistance fighters in Gaul, and his unambiguous anti-Roman stance, persuaded other like-minded groups to flock to his side. On the other hand his neighbours, the Trinovantes of Essex, had been calling on Rome to do something about him for many years. There was little love between them. Caesar's victory was thus significant, and it may have persuaded him he had done enough to subjugate this troublesome territory.

Caesar also received the delegations of several tribes, including the Cenimagni. He issued dire warnings of what would happen if anyone stepped out of line again, gathered together some hostages, fixed the rate of tribute (tax) to be paid annually to Rome, and once again returned to Gaul. Later, he was to write down his impressions of this strange land and its even stranger inhabitants. He was fascinated, among other things, by the tribal use of chariots. In Roman terms, these were an out of date form of equipment which by this time were used simply for racing.

Ultimately, of course, the taxes were not paid. The Catuvellauni rediscovered their composure and their troublesome ways, and within fifty years they had established a capital at the old Trinovantian centre at Colchester. As time slipped by a trickle of British pro-Roman kings, leaders and envoys appeared in Rome, as refugees, imploring the emperors to intervene once more.

A period of peace

Neither of Caesar's successors, Augustus and Tiberius, considered it an appropriate time to engage in an expedition to Britain. In AD 39—40 the Emperor Gaius Caligula did think about invasion once again, and he actually got as far as assembling a force at Boulogne. However, he was unable to persuade the troops to obey the embarkation instructions. Eventually, and on his orders, they threw their javelins into the sea and filled their helmets with seashells, which apparently was sufficient for Caligula to be able to claim a victory — over the ocean!

Caesar's expeditions did open the way for increased trade and served to draw Britain into the mainstream events of the Roman world. Sailing from ports in Gaul, traders soon began to penetrate the south, and they quickly forged a substantial presence. As the uneasy years passed, their familiarity and influence, and the popularity of their goods, grew and grew.

When Caesar launched his initial attacks on Gaul an already established pattern of trade between the Mediterranean world, Gaul and the south-west of Britain, was interrupted. When trade restarted after his two visits, the focus shifted further east, especially to the Thames estuary, Hertfordshire, Essex and Kent. Classical writers record that traders imported mainly luxury items including wine in large amphorae. They listed the British exports as corn, hides, slaves and hunting dogs. No doubt the traders also brought with them news and fresh ideas, new fads and fashions, and a fresh grasp of what lay beyond the ocean. It is certainly possible that some southern tribal leaders, in glimpsing a gradual erosion of the old ways and old standards, saw trouble ahead. Some may even have entertained the idea that a fragmented tribal system of warring kings and warrior bands was not the best way to withstand the strength and organisation of this mighty Empire.

These decades also saw a steady development of trade involving the Iceni. Trade routes were developing between the Thames area and northern East Anglia, and there is also clear evidence of direct contact between the Iceni and the tribes of northern Gaul. The nature of the imports did not tend to include the amphorae seen further south, but foreign coinage and metalwork was finding its way into the land of the Iceni. Rome, at last, was beginning to have an influence on the communities living in northern East Anglia.

Different peoples living across the south of Britain responded to these new developments in different ways. On the one hand, some were clearly fearful of the Roman military might which watched and waited on the other side of the Channel. They may have worried about a gradual erosion of the traditional ways and wondered what the future might hold. On the other hand, some loved the new goods and fashions, and clamoured to buy more. They now drank Roman wine from fine Roman silver cups, adopted Roman writing, and even began to give their children Roman names. It was becoming an invasion in all but name, and it was surely only a matter of time before the legions returned.

And return they did, of course, in AD 43.

Times

Tales of vulnerability

Although in many ways life continued as it had for generations, Roman traders were achieving increasing success in introducing their wares to the southern British tribes. The steady spread and acceptance of a Roman lifestyle was popularising new fashions, introducing new ideas and widening horizons. At the same time there was, even in parts of the south, a body of anti-Roman sentiment which at its fanatical and perhaps Druidic edge amounted to outright opposition. Opinion, it seems, was becoming polarised.

In the years following Caesar's withdrawal, rumours of Roman military vulnerability started to circulate. The event which sparked this astonishing situation occurred in AD 9 and it arose through the Emperor Augustus' affirmed policy towards the establishment of a northern frontier along the river Elbe. The XVII, the XVIII and the XIX Legions, under the command of Publius Quinctilius Varus, were lured deep into the hinterland of the Teutoburger forest where they were ambushed by the Cherusci tribe led by Arminius. The loss of 30,000 men left a lasting psychological scar on the Romans. Tacitus wrote how Roman bones were later found scattered and whitening among the trees. It was a devastating and humiliating defeat, and Augustus was eventually forced to amend his policy and withdraw to the river Rhine. The hurt ran deep.

There were further concerns for the Romans in the north-western empire centred around the priesthood. The Druids are thought to have played a major political role in focusing and uniting native resistance to Rome. This, together with the alleged savagery of their priestly rites, led the Romans to oppose their cult. During the revolt of Florus and Sacrovir in Gaul, action was taken to stamp them out. Some of the Gaulish Druidic leaders, however, managed to flee to Britain to provide yet another shot in the arm for the British anti-Roman faction.

Meanwhile, political power in Britain was beginning to shift. Somewhere between AD 40 and 43, at a time when Boudica may have been a young girl, there occurred the death of Cunobelinus. He had been king of the often war-like Catuvellauni, who had ruled large parts of southern England for over thirty years. Instability quickly followed his death, for his legacy was a tribal territory divided between his two young and equally troublesome and war-like sons, Caratacus and Togodumnus.

Claudius became Roman Emperor in AD 41, and this time a decision was taken to invade Britain. He had made a difficult start to his reign and needed a victory to bolster his standing in Rome, military glory being almost an expectation at the time. With this in mind, success in Britain would not only allow him to emulate the feats of the great Julius Caesar, but an actual conquest would surpass the achievements of his illustrious predecessor. An invasion of Britain had other advantages for him, too, in that it would allow him to deal with the British mercenaries, who regularly opposed him in Gaul, as well as the Druids. Britain, too, as Gaulish merchants no doubt reported, was seen as being awash with grain, something needed by his legions in Gaul. There was, Claudius seems to have concluded, much to gain and little to lose.

Another deciding factor may have been that much of the groundwork for an invasion had already been completed by the staff of another of his predecessors, Gaius Caligula. Ships had already been built and coastal warehouses constructed. In this way Claudius was able to re-assemble the invasion force at Boulogne and other ports, wait for a fair wind, and set sail.

D-Day, AD 43

The invasion force under the overall command of Aulus Plautius consisted of four legions, each of 6,000 troops. These were the Legio II Augusta, Legio IX Hispana, Legio XIV Gemina and the Legio XX Valeria. There were also 20–30,000 auxiliary cavalry and infantry. Together, the army of invasion comprised some 50,000 fighting men. As Caligula had discovered three years earlier, mainland troops were reluctant to embark for this as yet largely unknown and unwelcoming land across a grey and rough sea, but Claudius was prepared for this, and his payment of a bonus soothed nerves. Nevertheless, the departure of the fleet was delayed and British tribes, lulled into believing the invasion had been abandoned, foolishly dispersed their forces.

The arrival off-shore of even the vanguard would have provoked extreme alarm among British coastal observers. This force of men, animals and stores must have created an enormous armada scattered widely over the Channel. As it was, the bulk of the force made an unopposed landing at Richborough, in the north-east corner of Kent, while another part of the invasion force landed near Fishbourne in Sussex, allowing the supply vessels to unload in safety. The army was accompanied by civil servants, support services, traders and a civilian retinue, which formed a very significant incursion of people into Britain.

The subjugation of Britain can never have been perceived as easy. The invasion and its aftermath, however, was to set Briton against Briton.

Bridging the gap

The initial phase of the conquest was rapid. After light skirmishes, Caratacus and Togodumnus fixed a rendezvous of the British forces at the River Medway. The British anticipated a lengthy Roman bridge-building operation, and they settled down on the far bank and waited, but this was their downfall. Special units of the invasion force trained in the art of wading rivers in full kit took the British by surprise. Under a flanking attack, the British hurriedly turned their chariots against the invaders who then reinforced their grip on the battlefield by shooting the horses and finishing the job in a fierce hand-to-hand confrontation. Then, with the tribes in disarray, Vespasian led the II Augusta over the river. The battle is said to have lasted all day and night and into the following morning. It ended with Togodumnus dead and in a decisive victory for Plautius.

The depleted British pulled back to the Thames, once again using a stretch of water as a defensive barrier, somewhere near present-day London. The second battle seems to have followed the pattern of the first in that some Roman troops in full gear waded or swam across the river to attack the British flank while the main Roman force crossed elsewhere by ford or bridge. Once again, the British were taken by surprise and suddenly found themselves fighting on at least two fronts.

At this point Plautius sent a despatch to Claudius in Rome. The Emperor immediately set sail, joined the invasion force at the Thames, and then led them across the river to attack the British who had assembled there. Claudius then led the legions on to Camulodunum where, greatly pleased, he accepted the submission of eleven tribes. This illustrious deed was later recorded on an arch erected in Rome in AD 51–52. In all, Claudius spent just sixteen days in his new territory, after which he received the title *Britannicus*.

Plautius moved immediately to extend the area of Roman military control.

The legions duly fanned out, with the II Augusta heading west, the XX Valeria marching towards the Welsh borders, the XIV Gemina moving into the Midlands, and the IX Hispana swinging east and then north.

The client kingdom

The Iceni were bestowed the status of client kingdom, which meant they were more or less free providing they stuck to all the rules laid down by Rome. Freedom from external interference was guaranteed by treaty. They were able to retain many of their own laws and traditions, as well as their own coinage. They were also largely exempt from the burden of having to pay tax and tribute, which other subjects of the Empire did. Assistance in the event of any external attack was also guaranteed by the Emperor. In return, a client king had to recognise that he ruled by courtesy of the Roman Emperor.

It was a system designed to ensure security on the boundaries of Roman rule. A client kingdom provided a 'buffer zone' in the event of external attack, and provided the Roman authorities with a cushion of time in which to respond. Initially, the Iceni appreciated the mutual benefits of this new system, and they remained peaceful.

A trading state

The Iceni had been steadily developing trading contacts both with other parts of Britain and further afield. In the years before the tribe was fully united the smaller sub-groups had undertaken exchange with each other, and with other people beyond the region. The use of coinage also developed steadily, and the larger sites in the south, especially Saham Toney, became thriving economic centres. Other settlements like Ditchingham developed on trade routes, especially in relation to the rivers. Some of these sites, like Crownthorpe and Great Walsingham, were to continue as major centres, developing into small towns in the Roman period.

In the decades before the Roman invasion trade increased further, and more non-Icenian coins are found in the area. Trade developed in the south with tribes in the Thames area, and to the west with the Corieltauvi. Simularities between the coins of these tribes and those of the Iceni bear evidence of these links. Icenian coastal trade also developed with other parts of Britain, and there were maritime links with northern France and the Low Countries.

More and more trading goods were manufactured and produced by the Iceni. In the years before Boudica's birth the larger sites in the south of the territory became increasingly prominent and prosperous as a result of trade. This success ultimately served to provide a political power base in Breckland and in other southern parts of the territory.

Early manoeuvres

Norfolk's early Roman military sites can be seen as part of a pattern of military garrisons situated across southern and eastern Britain. Forts are known from a number of locations, and they appear to have been placed in strategic locations adjacent to prominent native Icenian settlements.

One Claudian fort was constructed at Woodcock Hall, Saham Toney, on a bluff to the south of the River Blackwater. Others have been discovered through aerial photography, showing up as playing-card-shaped cropmarks. In 1984 one such fort was revealed at Swanton Morley, near Billingford, in central Norfolk. In 1996 yet another was revealed at Barton Bendish in the south-west, to the west of the Devil's Dyke earthwork. This example had been sited next to another important Late Iron Age settlement, at Fincham.

Much more evidence for the Roman army in Norfolk comes in the form of metalwork finds, which are widespread across the county. These items include tunic fittings, pieces of armour, weapons and coins, all used by the soldiers. There was a substantial demand for coins by the invading army, together with their associated civil servants, followers and traders, but there was no official mint in Britain at that time. To address the shortage, some coins were produced by the army. These were crude copies of coins of the Emperor Claudius, and they tend to be found at sites which have military associations.

Numerous military finds can also be associated with the Pye Road in east

Norfolk, in the vicinity of Scole, Caistor St Edmund and Horstead. Yet more have been found to the north of Thetford and all the way through to the area around Ashill and Threxton. Some other finds, especially coins, appear to be more closely associated with coastal locations, and it may be that the Roman navy played more of a role in subduing this area than has been appreciated in the past.

Pacifying the natives

For the Britons, the presence of foreign troops must have provoked the sort of feelings felt by all people trying to cope with an occupation. There must have been apprehension on the part of some, and loathing among others. Of course, they had seen Roman troops and traders before, but not with this weight of weaponry and certainly not this close.

Nevertheless, life for the Iceni went on as before even though the atmosphere was doubtless riven with argument, rumour and counter-rumour. After all, and despite the troops, there were still fields to be tilled, crops to be gathered, beer to be brewed and stock to be tended, herded, slaughtered and traded.

The first Iceni revolt

In about AD 47 Aulus Plautius was replaced as military commander, enabling him to return to Rome in triumph and be received by a delighted Claudius. His replacement was Ostorius Scapula, who brought with him specific orders to complete the conquest of Britain. Several trouble spots remained, notably related to Caratacus, who had gained control in the west and was still leading raiding parties based in Wales and the west Midlands. By AD 47, Scapula was clearly determined to launch a major offensive.

It is possible Scapula also felt a need to 'blood' some of the fresh troops sent to make up losses during the invasion phase. Even so, his real problem was still a basic shortage of men. Many of his cohorts were deployed in the four corners of the island, and there were few others available to form a new force. In consequence, he had little option but to draw on the garrisons of the forts, thus leaving some of the old tribal areas, particularly in the south-east, with no-one to keep watch on them. As a military man he was clearly and keenly aware of the potential for danger, and as a precautionary measure decided to enforce a Roman law, the *Lex Julia de Armis*, which effectively disarmed the native people.

The object of this law was to deprive tribes of their battle weapons while allowing them to keep hunting weapons and carry a weapon while travelling. But it seems to have provoked particular offence among factions of the Iceni elite. Perhaps some of them tried to turn the situation to their advantage, or saw an opportunity to catch Scapula off guard. What is known is that British Iron Age warriors had a special relationship with their weapons and would not wish be parted from them, even in death. Eventually, the resentment boiled over and some of the Iceni finally rebelled.

Scapula quickly realised that the revolt needed to be crushed. The rebels, perhaps expecting more support than they actually got, had little option but to retreat into a stronghold which, Tacitus tells us, was defended by earth banks and ditches and had a single line of approach along a narrow entrance. Tacitus did not record where it was, but two places within Iceni territory fit the description. Stonea was an isolated island in the middle of the flooded Cambridgeshire fens, while Holkham (north Norfolk), lay in an expanse of tidal saltmarsh.

Scapula mobilised a major force in order to ensure a swift conclusion, and in due course his troops appeared within sight of the Iceni defences. Noting the narrowness of the access route, he ordered his cavalry to dismount. The fort was stormed on foot, and the revolt was decisively crushed. A year later, in AD 48, Scapula was awarded the *Corona Civica* for bravery in battle.

The rise of Prasutagus

The years following this first uprising saw the unification, under Prasutagus, of the various Iceni factions spread across the region. We cannot be certain of the precise boundaries, but they came together to form a single tribal grouping which continued right through into the Roman period proper.

We know very little about
Prasutagus — who took as his bride
the lady known to history as Boudica
— but he is one of the few people
of the time of whom we do have a
contemporary image. After AD 47 the
Roman authorities allowed a small
coinage to be issued in his name
which carried his Romanised portrait
and which also symbolised the tribe's
positive relationship with Rome in
the aftermath of this first rebellion.

Silver coin of King Prasutagus.
Diameter 14mm.

The pro-Roman atmosphere
prevailing in the post-rebellion years saw Roman money-lenders move into
northern East Anglia. These included the representatives of Seneca and
Catus Decianus, and they met members of the Iceni ruling elite. Money in
the form of loans changed hands. This was a defining moment in the story,
for within thirteen years these same loans would become a major issue in the
confusion which eventually led to conflict. Quite simply, the Iceni were not
used to the concept of borrowing, and they received these sums, which were
wrapped in words of friendship, in the spirit of gift exchanges. Such a practice
was familiar to the Iceni as a way of confirming mutual respect. Of course, to
be asked to return items exchanged in this way would have been perceived as
a huge affront to the dignity of the entire tribe.

Soon after the first Iceni uprising a Roman *colonia*, or colony, was
established at Colchester. This was in about AD 49, and the colony was laid
out over the former legionary fortress. Retired army veterans were moved
in, being encouraged to settle there by the promise of land. The scheme,
however, caused great friction with the local population as the land in
question was simply being confiscated from those living in the surrounding
area. From the Roman point of view the plan to settle veterans in the area
was also seen as a safeguard; should there be any sort of emergency, then the
veterans could provide a sort of trained Home Guard.

In AD 48, Ostorius Scapula resumed his campaigns in the west of the
country. In AD 58 Suetonius Paulinus became governor, and it was during

his period in office that the catalyst for the Boudican uprising occurred. The trigger event was the death of Prasutagus, ruler of the Iceni, in AD 60.

Who was Boudica?

What do we know about Boudica? We have no details of her background or early life, but it is probable that she came from a prominent family within local society. She would certainly have been a refined woman, probably educated, and influenced by fashionable Roman fads and styles.

Where did she come from? At the time of her birth, northern East Anglia was a loose confederation of small family units, so it is conceivable that her marriage to Prasutagus might have come about in order to help strengthen ties between the factions within the Iceni, and bond the tribe together. It is also possible that she may have been born within the territory of the Iceni's western neighbours, the Corieltauvi, or among the Catuvellauni to the south. Again, such a scenario may have been seen as an attempt to bind together neighbouring peoples at a time of a perceived major external threat.

What did she look like? Dio refers to her as being tall. He also says she was 'of the royal family', and formidable in appearance, with a harsh voice and a mass of tawny hair which fell to her hips. Around her neck, he wrote, she wore a ceremonial gold necklace, possibly an ancestral torc, and a tunic of many colours. Over this was a thick cloak fastened with a brooch, which may have been one of the 'rear-hook' type, a style very popular with Iceni metalworkers. Her dress was probably influenced by Roman fashion and, as an aristocrat, she may even have used cosmetics. Many small hand-held 'cosmetic grinders', which were made for this purpose and are of the right date, have been found in Boudican territory.

And how old was she? Neither Cassius Dio nor Tacitus make reference to this, but we do know that in AD 60 she had two daughters who had reached the age

A cosmetic palette, designed to grind coloured powders for make-up, used by wealthy women at the time of Boudica. Length 59mm.

of puberty but were not yet married. If they were in their teen years then their dates of birth would have been during the years around AD 45. From this reasoning, we may suggest that Boudica was born around AD 25, making her about thirty-five at the time of her revolt.

The naming game

The name Boudica requires some explanation. Sources suggest there is a link between modern Gaelic and the ancient Celtic languages, in both of which the name *bouda* translates as 'victory'. In modern Welsh the closest word is *buddug*. So the name of the Iceni leader, Boudica, translates as 'Victoria'. A form of this name has also been found in mainland Europe. In 1921 an altar to a goddess called Tetula Boudiga, 'the victorious', was unearthed at Bordeaux.

Portrait of Boudica, painted by Ivan Lapper; based on the description by the Roman historian Dio Cassius.

In fact the spelling of the name in this book is not the one used by Tacitus. He called her Boudicca, mistakenly adding an additional 'c'. The error was then compounded by a medieval copyist working on the Tacitus text. He inscribed an 'a' instead of a 'u' and an 'e' instead of the second 'c', resulting in 'Boadicea'. Poetically minded Victorians seized upon this version of the name, which has endured to this day with many people. However, the most correct version of the spelling is Boudica.

Writings and reminiscences

We are fortunate to have surviving accounts by a number of classical writers who recorded aspects of the period surrounding the lifetime of Boudica. A most valuable source for the general period is Julius Caesar himself, who left us a history known as *The Gallic Wars*, which pre-dates the rebellion but does provide some source material about Britain and the British.

None of the writings which refer to the actual Boudican revolt are contemporary. They were written long after the event and were also compiled from the perspective of the eventual victors. Gaius Suetonius, born about AD 69, wrote *The Twelve Caesars*. He dealt with the period in a very few words, but his book includes useful quotations and remarks about the Emperors Claudius, Nero and Vespasian. However, the two most significant writers in terms of Boudica's uprising were Cassius Dio and Tacitus.

Cassius Dio was a Greek, born about AD 150, nearly a century after the actual rebellion. In AD 180 he went to Rome, entered the Senate, and became the confidant of several emperors. He held several important positions, becoming Consul and then Proconsul of Africa. He died in AD 235, leaving behind a collection of written work known as his *Roman History*, much of which was subsequently lost. Fortunately, the volumes relating to the early occupation of Britain are among those which do survive, though his references are also brief.

Dio may also have had the works of another writer at his elbow as he worked. This was perhaps the most significant commentator of them all, the Roman historian Tacitus (born AD 56—57, died AD 118). Tacitus married a daughter of Iulius Agricola, who had been an officer in the Roman army at the time of the Boudican rebellion, and who later became Governor of Britain in AD 78, eighteen years after the rebellion. Although writing some fifty years after the event, Tacitus would have benefited from listening to Agricola's first-hand, eye-witness accounts. Tacitus may also have had access to Imperial documents and spoken to other military veterans of the British campaign.

In AD 97, shortly after the death of the Emperor Domitian, Tacitus attained a Consulship and later became Governor of the province of western Anatolia (modern Turkey). It was in the following year that he began his career as a historian. *The Annals* covers Roman history from AD 14 to the death of Nero in AD 68, and it provides us with most of the detail of the events surrounding the rebellion.

Confrontation

Paulinus was planning a major attack on Anglesey — the final stronghold of the Druids and their followers — which had become the last real focus of British resistance. It was at this moment that Prasutagus passed away. He had made plans to leave his estate, on his death, to be shared between the Emperor, Nero, and his own daughters. It was a naive and fateful decision, because a Roman emperor did not share with anyone.

At the same time, Seneca decided to call in his loans, a move which was to cause the Romans unforeseen problems. The British simply did not understand the nature of loans, and they had seen the exchanges as outright gifts. Thus the stage was set for an explosive conclusion.

The task of the Procurator was to enforce the authority of the Emperor, and Decianus applied himself to the job with vigour. Troops and administrators moved into Iceni territory to take back the region for the Emperor. Boudica, no doubt, was reluctant to hand anything to these arrogant Romans, and so it became a situation pregnant with danger. When something did go wrong, violence quickly flared.

Decianus and his followers clearly felt they could act with impunity. Boudica was flogged and her daughters raped. It was an attack not only on them as women but also on the royal house of the Iceni, and thus on the entire tribe. The event was particularly devastating to the Iceni as they had considered themselves allies of Rome. Had they not signed a treaty? Did they not have client kingship? Were the Romans not supposed to be their partners? Had they not exchanged gifts?

The place where these atrocities occurred is likely to have been at or near one of the major tribal centres, which could have been Caistor St Edmund or perhaps Thetford or Saham Toney. Boudica — who was not described as a queen in ancient sources, but merely as a wife — suffered the agonies of a wounded mother and, calling on all of her courage and strength, she duly demanded vengeance.

Island diplomacy

Boudica knew that Roman military attention was focused elsewhere. Paulinus was absorbed in his campaign in north Wales, no doubt believing that the legions and veterans to his rear were quite capable of dealing with any minor problems that might arise. Boudica, however, would have found instant allies within the Trinovantes, who had a simmering resentment over the loss of their land given to Roman veterans around Colchester. They were also angry over the construction of a temple dedicated to the sacred cult of Claudius at the *colonia*.

The revolt of AD 60 should not be seen as a nationwide rebellion. Support for Boudica was regional, and limited to East Anglia; the south remained largely indifferent to the plight of the Iceni. However, Dio provides a figure of 120,000 rebels, which constitutes the largest enemy force the Romans had encountered in Britain. Dio also says that Boudica herself directed the conduct of the war.

In a manner typical of classical writers, Dio related a long speech given by Boudica to her army. In it, he says, she described how her people had been deceived 'by the alluring promises of the Romans'. She concluded: 'How much better is poverty with no master than wealth with slavery.' She then released a hare from the folds of her dress which, as it ran away, proved to the people that the omens were good. Then, with arms raised, she called upon Andraste to help their cause.

On the other side of the country, on the Isle of Anglesey, Paulinus was initially unaware of these developments. The object of his immediate concern faced him on the far shoreline where he and his troops could see hordes of warriors being encouraged and urged on by the frenzy of priests. He knew he faced a fierce battle against the Druids, who were fighting for their way of life as well as their lives.

Intercept mission

The uprising took place during late spring or early summer, and Iceni farmers would not have completed their seasonal planting. So the stakes were high on all counts, for failure ending in defeat would also mean starvation. However, the rebels, accompanied by their wagons and carts, streamed

© Sue White

south. Boudica's rebel army was now swollen by fighters from other tribes, and the horde took to the road with the clear intention of launching a strike against the Romans. Colchester was the Roman regional capital, and their cultural showpiece. It was also populated by army veterans and civilians, but had no garrison. And it was the place where the authorities were busily building their temple dedicated to the spirit of Claudius. The destruction of

Colchester would gladden the hearts of all those wanting vengeance against the new rulers.

Rumours of the revolt and the unexpected movement of so many people meant the rebellion could not go undetected for long. Word quickly reached the ears of Petillius Cerialis, legate of the IX Hispana Legion stationed at Longthorpe, near Peterborough. Cerialis immediately grasped the seriousness of the situation and mobilised a detachment of his troops, perhaps seeking to undertake a reconnaissance. However, he marched straight into an ambush. Boudica may have been informed of these movements, or she may have anticipated the move. Either way, the whole Roman infantry force, numbering 1,500 men, were caught and slaughtered, and Cerialis and his surviving cavalry had little option other than to retreat back to Longthorpe.

There was a further setback for the Roman military command. Cerialis, by now understanding that the situation was critical, rushed messages to Paulinus in Anglesey and to the II Legion in its fortress at Exeter. The II

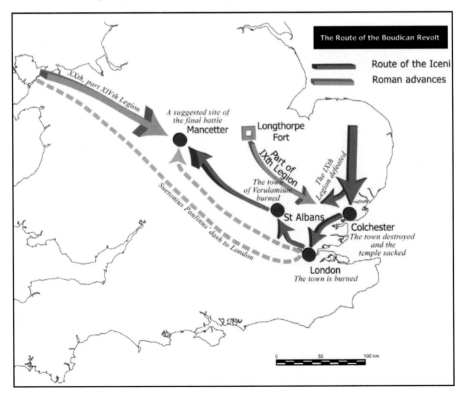

The Route of the Boudican Revolt

Route of the Iceni
Roman advances

XXth, part XIVth Legion

A suggested site of the final battle
Mancetter

Longthorpe Fort

Part of IXth Legion

The IXth Legion defeated

Suetonius Paulinus' dash to London

The town of Verulamium burned

St Albans

Colchester
The town destroyed and the temple sacked

London
The town is burned

0   50   100 km

Legion was at that time commanded by a prefect named Poenius Postumus, an elderly soldier on the verge of retirement. Postumus decided not to respond, but to keep his troops safely in their base. Perhaps he feared a local uprising, or concluded that a march through a southern England on the verge of war was just too dangerous. The effect was that the II Legion missed out on the chance of battle honours and loot, and eventually the disgraced Postumus chose to fall on his sword. Decianus, unnerved by the revolt he had been instrumental in causing, fled to Gaul.

Temple of doom

Slowly the noose tightened on Colchester. The *colonia* was virtually defenceless, and rumour and counter-rumour swept the town. Finally, when a rebel attack seemed inevitable, an appeal was made to Decianus — who may still have been in London — to send assistance. By that stage, however,

Boudica's horde pours into Colchester: illustration by Jamel Akib.

Colchester is savagely destroyed by Boudica's army: illustration by Jamel Akib.

all Decianus could or would muster was a wholly inadequate force of 200 poorly armed men.

The defenders of Colchester may now have numbered about 3,000. The records suggest they fought doggedly, but to no avail, and they eventually fell back to the solidarity of the uncompleted stone temple to make their final stand. Finally, the temple itself was razed, and a massacre began. Thousands died. The destruction of the *colonia* was as devastating as it was total.

Evidence of the battle still survives today. Below some of the present streets and buildings of Colchester there is a layer of black scorched earth, much of it containing the burnt remains of personal possessions. Such was the fierceness of the fires that buildings baked into clay, timbers were charred, mattresses carbonised, cups and bowls melted into puddles of glass, and glossy red samian ware pottery burned black. Even the charred remains of fruits — dates, plums and figs — have been found in archaeological deposits.

Two Roman military tombstones which had been hacked and damaged by Boudica's rebels were found to the south of the main road leading out of Colchester towards London. One had commemorated Longinus, an officer of the First Thracian cavalry regiment, and the other a centurion of the XX Legion called M. Favonius Facilis.

Yet more evidence of the destruction of Colchester has come from very surprising locations further north, in Suffolk and Norfolk. In 1907 a bronze

Head of the emperor Claudius; part of the Roman equestrian statue at Colchester, removed by the Iceni. Found in the River Alde, Suffolk. BELOW RIGHT: *Fragment in the shape of a horse's knee, found at Ashill in central Norfolk; length 356mm.* BELOW: *Reconstruction of the whole statue, showing the positions of the surviving fragments.*

head of Claudius, once part of a much larger statue, was found in the river Alde near Saxmundham in Suffolk. Jagged edges around the neck provided clear evidence that it had been removed by force. This was later recognised as part of the equestrian statue that had stood outside the temple of Claudius when the rebels entered Colchester. It had clearly been removed as loot by one of Boudica's warriors on his way back home. Then, in 1979, another statue fragment was discovered in Norfolk, 37 miles (60 km) away from Saxmundham. This time it was a fragment of the knee of a horse. It was made of the same metal alloy and had been part of the same statue from the temple of Claudius. This time the findspot was at Ashill, in Norfolk, part of the Saham Toney *oppidum* and some 43 miles (69 km) from Colchester. Could this have been a souvenir brought back to Norfolk by a returning Iceni warrior?

Return of Paulinus

Boudica now turned her thoughts to the next stage of the campaign and decided to attack London, which symbolised Roman rule and the new way of life. London had been a Roman foundation and its existence was based on Roman trade. Just as today, it was a financial centre and a city of businessmen and, as such, it epitomized the new Roman administration. It was a prime target for Iceni wrath. London was also a growing town with an increasing strategic importance, and the fact that it was not fortified and virtually undefended again made it a soft target.

Paulinus is said to have received news of the East Anglian uprising at the very moment he and his troops were savouring victory against the Druids on the island of Anglesey. He grasped the implications immediately and cut short the mopping-up operation. Instead, he ordered his troops to march south, and raced towards London — about 250 miles away — along Watling Street, which follows the line of the modern A5 road.

Meanwhile, Boudica's horde straggled towards the Thames. Chelmsford was then a minor settlement located at the crossing point of the Colchester to London road over the River Can. Evidence for a fire dated to about this time has been found, but it is unclear whether this can be associated with the rebellion. In fact, Tacitus tells us that Boudica avoided forts and garrisons on her way south, and an early fort has been excavated at Chelmsford.

The journey south may have taken Paulinus the best part of a week, but even so he seems to have arrived at his destination before Boudica and her rebels. Boudica may simply have been uncertain how to exploit the victory at Colchester, or undecided what to do next. Paulinus, however, grasped matters quickly. London's business and trading centre was around the Walbrook stream and covered what is now the City of London. There was also a small suburb sited in present day Southwark, south of the river Thames. The settlement, in general, was a mass of narrow, crowded streets, with a population of about 30,000.

With the main body of his troops still several days' march away, Paulinus realised that a defence of London was impossible. What was needed to crush the rebels was a set-piece confrontation on a battlefield of his choosing, and not the chaos of hand-to-hand combat in crowded streets amid burning buildings. In consequence, he brushed aside the pleadings of merchants and their families and withdrew towards the Midlands.

The destruction levels beneath present day London testify to the level of brutality which now engulfed those of the terrified community who had not managed to flee. The burnt layer, some thirteen feet down, is 17 inches (40 cm) thick. The sources describe savage atrocities, particularly against Roman women, which demonstrate the depth of feeling surrounding the earlier violation of the Iceni royal family.

Even Southwark did not escape Boudica's fury. Excavation in advance of the Jubilee Line extension at Borough High Street discovered a series of timber buildings, built about AD 50—55, which were also destroyed. In Fenchurch Street, during further excavation of the Boudica layer, a mass of burned cereal was discovered. This included bitter vetch and einkorn. The latter had been imported into Britain, providing fascinating evidence that there had been a poor or even a failed harvest during the year prior to the revolt.

Paulinus, meanwhile, carefully made his preparations as he waited for the main body of his troops to arrive from Anglesey, and thus the stage was set for the decisive confrontation.

Arms and the men

It is possible that Boudica was not in complete control of her army at this point. Perhaps it was blood lust, religious fervour, or simple exhilaration that drove her army forward. But advancing towards a set-piece battle rather than opting for a guerrilla-style campaign clearly turned the tide in favour of Paulinus. An advantage in numbers was one thing, but an advantage in weaponry, tactics and discipline was quite another.

Boudica and her warriors streamed north in the Romans' wake towards Verulamium (near modern St Albans). Before the Claudian invasion this had been an Iron Age community and it had developed quickly under Roman influence. It became a *municipium*, which was an urban centre second only in status to a *colonia*, containing a fusion of native and Roman lifestyles. Boudica treated the place as she had treated Colchester and London, and Verulamium was destroyed, along with some neighbouring farmsteads. This time, though,

The sack of Verulamium: painting by John Pearson.

some of the inhabitants managed to flee, carrying their portable belongings.

The impending confrontation was to be between two very different armies. Boudica's force, which according to Dio may have swelled to about 230,000, was made up of largely undisciplined individuals who fought for honour and freedom. Their bodies were unprotected by armour. Instead, they wore leather trousers, while their arms and trunks were decorated by designs daubed in blue dye. They carried a wooden, leather or bronze oval shield which reached from the chin to the knees, and their main battle weapon was the spear, a fearsome seven- or eight-foot (over 2 metres) weapon with an iron spearhead. Many of them also carried a flat, double-edged sword, about three feet (0.9 m) long. Some rode chariots. These vehicles were light, fast carts with slender wheels, pulled by two ponies and usually driven by a slave or servant. By and large, chariots were no longer in use on the Continent, and Roman troops may have been amazed to be faced by what they thought of as yesterday's war technology.

Opposing this fanatical host was the much smaller Roman army which numbered about 10,000 battle-hardened and disciplined men. They comprised the XIV Legion, with detachments of the XX Legion and auxiliaries drawn from nearby garrisons. The Roman infantryman wore a helmet, body armour, thick belt and leather apron. Each carried a shield edged with bronze with an iron boss in the centre. Each man also carried two javelins, over six feet long, and a short stabbing sword called a *gladius*. Their tactics, discipline and ability to fight in tight battle units made this a fighting force without equal in the ancient world.

Final curtain

It is possible that Paulinus already knew the place where he wanted to make his stand, and he may even have passed it by on his journey south from Anglesey. We know that the selected location was part of a range of hills offering an open space with thick woods behind and on either side. There was also a view over where Watling Street crossed a river in a wide, marshy valley. Dio's description of the battlefield closely matches a spot near Mancetter, in Warwickshire, though the battle site remains a matter for continued debate.

By the time Boudica and her rebels arrived they would have seen lines of Roman troops in battle formation in the distance, with the legions positioned in the centre and the auxiliary cavalry on either side.

Whatever their thoughts on the eve of battle, many of Boudica's host must have realised they had reached a point of no return. They would defeat the Roman occupation force now, or not at all. The battle would decide everything, and confidence, whether raised by religious fervour or by blood lust, clearly welled through their veins. When the time came the rebels attacked in the only way they knew, with a full-on assault.

First, they had to struggle through the marshes and across the shallow river, and progress was slow. One can imagine the mass of warriors beginning to falter and becoming scattered even before they came within range of Roman weaponry. In this action they were watched and encouraged by their wives and families who were lined up behind the advance as part of the baggage train. Then the first flight of Roman javelins whistled through the air,

The East Midlands town of Mancetter is regarded as a prime candidate for the final battle because of the lay of the land. BELOW: *Illustrations by Jamel Akib.*

causing further delay and confusion. Seizing the moment, Suetonius then let his lines of armoured infantrymen off the leash, and slowly and methodically they moved downhill. Battle proper was joined.

The rebel army, already slowed and confused, was unprepared to meet this attack. The legionaries soon made substantial inroads, hacking their way forward, dividing the Iceni and their allies into fragmented groups and bringing slaughter to the field. In the end, it was a massacre. The Roman lines moved methodically onwards and the rebels fell back; so far back, in fact, that they now became trapped among their own wagons and by the presence of the women and children. There was no mercy. The Romans slaughtered all before them, and many of those who attempted to escape the mêlée were chased and cut down by the cavalry.

Roman victory was complete. Tacitus records that about 80,000 Iceni and their allies were killed, with just 400 Roman lives lost. Although these figures may have been distorted for the benefit of a Roman readership, the scale of the defeat is clear. This was perhaps the defining moment which cleared the way for a further three-and-a-half centuries of Roman occupation in Britain.

Those rebels who did manage to escape the slaughter attempted to make their way home, though it could not have been an easy journey. Anyone of fighting age would have been viewed as a probable refugee and enemy, and Paulinus would have searched out anyone who might have inflamed a future revolt.

The astonishing discovery of two fragments of the equestrian statue of Claudius deposited in Suffolk and in Norfolk has already been mentioned. If these items were indeed looted as souvenirs by participants in the battles, then it is not surprising that they were secretly buried. Roman retribution

on those caught in possession of such items would doubtless have been merciless. However, it is fascinating to consider that some warriors did survive the battles and evidently lived to return to their native homeland.

Boudica seems to have fled the battlefield, for both Tacitus and Cassius Dio agree she died later. Perhaps she fled when she saw the rebel advance falter amid a rain of javelins, or as the lines of Roman infantrymen advanced down the hill. Perhaps her advisers begged her to flee. Tacitus wrote that she committed suicide by taking poison, whereas Dio reports that she died following an illness. Suicide was probably her only option. With the bulk of her warriors killed and hunting parties combing the countryside for survivors, her first instinct may have been to avoid capture. Perhaps she might have hidden for a time in the vast fenland around the Wash. However, there were few places to which she might have fled. The pro-Roman population would have been only too happy to hand her over to the authorities, and the Romans would have been watching the ports. Her instinct would have been to avoid being taken back to Rome in chains and exhibited as a prize in a cruel triumph before being ceremonially executed. When she died, Dio relates that it was in a lavish ceremony.

Folk stories relating to her final resting place range from Garboldisham, in Norfolk, to Hampstead Heath, London, and even King's Cross railway station. No one knows, and within a generation or two of the revolt everyone seems to have forgotten. Today, the finding of Boudica's grave is the prize every archaeologist dreams of winning.

Punishment and peace

The ending of the revolt brought Roman troops swarming back into the area that Scapula had stripped of men and weaponry some ten years before. Tacitus says the army stayed 'under canvas', which indicates they spent the winter on campaign, shivering in tents and temporary forts rather than in permanent barracks. Suspected ringleaders were rounded up. Starvation was another consequence for the Icenian survivors, for no crops had been planted the previous spring.

Friendlier factions of the Iceni who had not taken part in the revolt

The 2009 archaeological dig at Venta Icenorum took place to the south of the main site, to help establish the development of the area.

provided the beginnings of a new Roman power base, and the authorities now made a conscious choice for the location of their new *civitas capital*. They chose to favour the population living at Caistor St Edmund, which is located three miles south of modern Norwich, and gave the settlement there the name *Venta Icenorum*. The town went on to become the major Roman town in northern East Anglia. At the same time, they turned their backs on the prominent Late Iron Age Breckland settlements at Thetford and Saham Toney. Neither of these subsequently developed into a significant Roman settlement.

A number of the early Roman forts probably relate to this period, including one at Threxton and also the marching camp at Horstead, which was identified from the air as a large cropmark. Artefacts from the centre of Caistor St Edmund confirm a military presence there, too, before the town was built. Additional evidence again comes from aerial photography, which has shown triple ditches of military type running roughly parallel to the later town walls on the south and east sides. The area enclosed by the Caistor ditches is approximately that of a full-sized legionary base. It may be that a large force was temporarily stationed there at this time.

A dispute eventually arose between Julius Classicianus, the new procurator or financial controller, and Paulinus. There was a growing concern that Paulinus was displaying excessive ferocity in his mopping-up operations. Classicianus may have been worried about a possible drop in taxation income following the number of casualties among the Iceni and the Trinovantes. He may also have considered that most native revolts against the authority of Rome were sparked by excessive oppression, and what was needed was a more softly-softly approach. In any event, the dispute reached the ears of Nero who sent a civil servant, a Greek named Polyclitus, to settle the matter. Paulinus was replaced as Governor shortly afterwards.

Recovery and reconciliation

Perhaps modern Iraq provides an example of what might have happened in the aftermath of the revolt. During the Iraq War, Allied forces killed or captured some of the ringleaders of the old regime and spent time trying to crush all signs of resistance. At the same time, innocents were caught in the crossfire. But the Iraqi people and their way of life continued to survive even amid the wreckage of their former lives and as the violence – followed by new ideas and fashions from the West – lapped around them.

After the Boudica revolt the take-up of Roman fashions and styles was fairly rapid and, in some areas of the country, extraordinarily fast. However, native culture was never fully submerged. It was to resurface again, especially at times of crisis and stress, when some of the old sacred places were also to be used again. Native round houses did not disappear overnight, either, for some of the old ways managed to continue outside of the Roman towns. Indeed, some elements of Iron Age culture managed to outlast the Roman occupation of Britain. But a slow sea change must have been taking place. Very slowly, native rituals and designs began to be perceived as something associated with older people as new prosperity and the Roman Empire took over.

And as the generations rolled on so memories of Boudica, her deeds and her grave, as well as all physical remains, disappeared from the collective memory until only the silence of history remained.

Legacy

A memory etched deep and far

The story of Boudica has lived on over the centuries and through countless generations. It may, at first, have been suppressed following the initial wave of retribution inflicted on the Iceni rebels and their supporters who survived the final battle. And yet perhaps it was as a result of this that the tales actually survived and became a rallying call whenever injustice was faced. The story of Boudica later became synonymous with courage and struggle against the odds. In other words, she was reconstructed as a champion, personifying strength in adversity. Perhaps, perversely, the more negative association of glory in defeat does tend to strike a sympathetic chord with the British character. The British public will always clamour to champion the cause of the under-dog, as can be seen at any FA Cup Final or other major sporting event today.

Despite a gap of nearly two thousand years since her death, Boudica still remains at the forefront of the public imagination. As a leader perceived to have done her duty at a time of need, she strikes an instant historical chord. She is recalled again at the very moment there is a threat to be faced or some brave deed to be celebrated, and her memory is certainly forever associated with a feisty brand of stubbornness, tenacity, individuality and bravery. As the centuries progressed, memories of the true story of her struggle merged with myth.

For some years after the final battle of AD 61 her memory was celebrated

and her passing mourned by some, though probably in muted secrecy, while
recollections of her were recalled with bitterness by the Roman authorities.
Then, as the generations slipped away, she must have become little more
than a whispered recollection, and may even have been forgotten altogether
for a while.

We know that a limited memory of Boudica survived, at least in the
closeted sanctuary of scholarly imagination. This is shown in the writing of
Gildas, a monk, who was writing in the sixth century. Gildas wrote a learned
treatise in Latin, which can be translated as *The Ruin of Britain*, in which he
mentions the Boudican revolt. The Venerable Bede, too, writing from the
northern monastery of Jarrow, published his *Ecclesiastical History of England*
in AD 731, in which he tells how Britain was nearly lost to the Romans.

Another reference came from a Welsh ecclesiastic and antiquary named
Nennius, who between AD 796 and about AD 830 compiled his *Historia
Britonum*. Nennius mentions the revolt, though not Boudica herself. His
writing merges history with legend, and he also became enamoured with the
story of King Arthur.

Boudica was more properly 'rediscovered' as public property during the
Renaissance. The Italian writer Polydore Vergil, born in Urbino, was sent to
England by Pope Alexander VI. His *Anglica Historica* was written about 1512,
drawing on the writings of Tacitus and Dio Cassius. Vergil became somewhat
confused as a result of their different Greek and Latin spellings (Voadicia
from Tacitus, and Bonduica from Dio), and he subsequently wrote of her as
two separate people!

Hector Boece, who was born in Dundee about 1465, wrote his *History of
Scotland* in 1527. His account, once again, was very confused and managed
to combine the story of Boudica with that of Cartimandua of the Brigantes.
Boece compounded his confusion by transferring the homeland of Norfolk's
queen and her tribe some 200 miles north, near the Scottish border. He
also called her Queen Voada and gave her a younger daughter named
Vodicia, who had a brother called Corbrede, King of the Scots. Scotland
was a separate kingdom at this time, and Boece was portraying his central
heroine as a champion of national rights opposing external aggression. This
association was to be carried forward through various English writers during
the sixteenth century.

The revival of interest in Boudica was well under way when, about AD 1577, Ralph Holinshed produced his *Chronicles*. Although drawing heavily on Boece as a source, Holinshed's Queen Voada was at least brought south once more in a colourful drama which made much of the ferocity of the events while developing the daughters as major characters. Boudica herself was portrayed as a champion of liberty. She is illustrated within the work in sixteenth century dress, bearing a very close resemblance to contemporary portraits of Elizabeth I as depicted on her coinage. Holinshed goes as far as to describe her appearance as having a

> *Mighty tall personage, comlie shape, sever countenance, and sharp voice, with hir long and yellow tresses of heare reaching downe to hir thighs.*

An even more important moment in public awareness and understanding came in 1591 when Sir Henry Savile's translations of Tacitus' *Annals* and *Agricola* finally appeared in the English language. This was at a time when comparisons with Elizabeth I were becoming irresistible, and the theme of Boudica and her exploits was also mentioned and written about by Edmund Spenser, Ben Jonson, John Speed, John Milton, John Aubrey and William Camden, in his *Britannia* of 1586. By the end of the sixteenth century, however, historical research was beginning to develop into a discipline we would recognise today. Scholars were involved in a search for accurate information, and sought less to develop their accounts through colourful decoration. In this way, it was Camden who managed to link Boudica, and the Iceni, with Norfolk.

However, Boudica still remained a figure of interest and inspiration in the field of literature. The poet Edmund Spenser's eulogy to her, under the title *The Faerie Queene*, was published in 1590. His romantic account described Boudica as a true heroine, displaying great courage and acting as an example of patriotism. Then in 1614 the dramatist John Fletcher produced a theatrical drama called *Bonduca*. It was in 1782 that William Cowper, who is buried at East Dereham in central Norfolk, wrote his epic poem *Boadicea: An Ode*. Cowper related the story and its theme of patriotism to the political problems of his day, namely, the question of British territorial expansion and the troublesome American Independence movement. Two of Cowper's lines read:

> *Regions Caesar never knew*
> *Thy Posterity shall sway*

Thereafter, Boudica was firmly established in the national collective memory as our greatest national heroine. Cowper's words, of course, ultimately adorned the plinth of one of London's most enduring statues, depicting Boudica and her daughters.

By the middle years of the nineteenth century, Thomas Thorneycroft was working on his statue, later titled *Boadicea and her Daughters*, which was to be placed on the Embankment in central London. Thorneycroft's depiction was a very romantic image. We now know that his Roman-style chariot with its dramatic scythed wheels are inaccurate in archaeological terms, and have served to mislead generations of schoolchildren. However, at the time he sculpted the group no Iron Age chariot burial had been found in Britain for Thorneycroft to copy.

Time of empire

During the nineteenth century Boudica, who had become Boadicea in popular literature, was still being used as a figure of patriotism, heroism and nationalism in all forms of art, and as the British Empire expanded so her image was adapted to characterise what were promoted as the great British attributes.

In 1864 Alfred Lord Tennyson published his poem, *Boadicea*, which was a much more critical portrayal of an essentially violent heroine. Then in 1868 Charles Dickens wrote a children's story which retold the heroic story of the Iceni revolt, although naturally enough he skated over the darker episodes of the story. When Queen Victoria died in 1901 Marie Trevelyan had just published her book, *Britain's Greatness Foretold: The Story of Boadicea, the British Warrior Queen*. This contained yet another story of Boudica, portraying her as a great national heroine and a truly inspirational figure.

In 1896 Thorneycroft's statue was presented to the Nation and placed beside Westminster Bridge, where it still stands today. Its back is turned towards the location of the old Roman town, while it faces towards today's

Thorneycroft's statue of Boudica stands beside Westminster Bridge in London.

more democratic form of government within the Houses of Parliament.

The timing of the unveiling of Thorneycroft's statue could not have been better, coming as it did as the British Empire reached its zenith and the Victorian age was drawing to an end. The statue's sentimental statement about Boadicea and her daughters echoed what many Britons must have felt at the time, for it characterised national pride in the achievements of a great queen faced by a foreign foe. A parallel was being drawn with Queen Victoria, who was involved in many foreign exploits. A second parallel was present with the names of both queens, both of which meant victory.

Into the modern world

During the early twentieth century, stories and history books aimed at children reflected Britain's colonial outlook on the world. Boudica was regularly employed for this purpose, as in Charles Doughty's mythical poem of 1906, *The Dawn In Britain*. Then, the growing suffragette movement understandably embraced her as a symbol of female bravery. Indeed, one of their rallies actually assembled in front of Thorneycroft's statue. At the subsequent banquet the menu carried a drawing of Boudica holding a banner with the legend, 'Votes for Women'. The memory of Boudica was called upon as a national symbol once again during the First World War when a stretch of the British defences on the Western Front was patriotically named the 'Boudicea Redoubt'.

Between 1913 and 1915 the sculptor J. Havard Thomas also produced a stunning marble statue of Boudica and her two daughters. The association of the queen had now transcended that of British folk heroine to become the embodiment of a great Celtic leader. Titled *'Buddug Boadicea'*, the statue was unveiled in Cardiff town hall in 1916 by Lloyd George as one of a series of the 'Heroes of Wales'. Boudica had become a symbol of resistance and resilience, but not for a united Britain, for now she had been claimed by the Celtic peoples of the British Isles.

It was during the 1930s that archaeological work began to focus on the evidence for the Boudican episode. Sir Mortimer Wheeler undertook excavation at Verulamium, and this was followed by the location of burnt layers at Sheepen (Colchester) by Hawkes and Hull. In 1937 Lewis Spence published a major historical study of Boudica called *Boadicea: Warrior Queen of the Britons*, which was misleading and inaccurate in many respects. He commented in the foreword that he had decided to stick to the 'old spelling' of her name because if he used the then more fashionable 'Boudicca' no-one would know of whom he was writing.

Seventeen years later, after World War 2, Rosemary Sutcliff produced *The Eagle of the Ninth*, a splendid children's story based on an imaginary history of the IX Legion which had been cursed by Boudica and which later disappeared north of the border. This work of fiction, which has endured to this day, is still available in bookshops.

In 1978, Graham Webster published his study *Boudica: The British Revolt Against Rome AD 60*, which led to something of a rebirth of interest. Then there appeared Plantagenet Somerset Fry's books, *Boudicca* and *Rebellion Against Rome*. In 1988 Antonia Fraser published *The Warrior Queens: Boadicea's Chariot*, in which she highlighted the distinction between the historical figure and the legendary heroine.

More recently, Paul Sealey has provided the important *The Boudican*

The statue of Boudica and her daughters in City Hall, Cardiff

Revolt Against Rome (1997), while in the realms of fiction the public has also devoured a powerful series by Manda Scott. Since 2000, major studies have included *Boudica Iron Age Warrior Queen* by Richard Hingley and Christina Unwin and the impressive *Boudica* by Vanessa Collingridge. Modern stories written especially for children have included *Boodicca and the Romans* by Tony Robinson. In all, there have been many books and many gallons of newspaper and magazine printing ink spilled in retellings of the story. And still they come.

On and on

The public's fascination has continued, and Boudica has consistently shown she can be whatever we want or need her to be. Today, she might be seen as an embodiment of queenly or motherly virtues like, for example, Queen Victoria. She could also symbolise fierce independence, single mindedness,

Young visitors enjoy the 'chariot ride' in the Boudica Gallery at Norwich Castle Museum.

OPPOSITE: *Marina Morgan in the Eastern Angles production of* Boudica's Babes.

and political strength of character, as Queen Elizabeth I or even Margaret Thatcher. As a fighter against injustice and oppression she may even parallel Hereward the Wake or Winston Churchill. In any event, she has become a talismanic character whose memory has joined a pantheon of other idealised male and female role-models who also include Maid Marion, Florence Nightingale and Edith Cavell. Much depends, it seems, on the politics, fashions and needs of the time.

In recent years, too, there have also been numerous films, television dramas, video tapes, school projects and, in Norfolk, the creation of a major permanent exhibition at the Castle Museum in Norwich. There is even a walking route named after her, 'Boudica's Way', which runs from Diss in south Norfolk to Norwich and takes in the Romano-British site at Caistor St Edmund.

Following our developing appetite for Boudica, many parts of Britain have also continued to lay claim to an association with her story. When

An Edwardian stained glass depiction of Boudica, in Colchester Town Hall

OPPOSITE: With a little help from the current fashion for 'Horrible Histories' and a unit in their school work, Boudica is alive and well in a Norfolk carnival.

questioned, the general public tend to associate the town of Colchester with her name, despite the fact that the time she spent there was just long enough to burn the place to the ground. A beautiful stained glass window depicting the bust of the great queen in warrior fashion adorns Colchester Town Hall today. Further afield, the personification of Boudica as a Celtic folk heroine and the unveiling of her statue in Cardiff has been described above. Sadly, few people today think to associate Boudica with the place where she actually lived. Boudica lived in Norfolk. Whether or not she was born within Icenian territory, she nevertheless spent her adult life here, and many of the events surrounding her story happened here, too.

There is also continuing discussion and speculation over her final resting place. Locations in various parts of the country have been suggested. Warlies Park in Essex is reported to have two eighteenth-century obelisks, one of which is said to mark the spot where Boudica took poison and the other where she died. Norfolk has two sites, both known locally as 'Boadicea's Grave', at Garboldisham and Quidenham. Meanwhile, and as recently as 1995, archaeologists in Birdlip (Gloucestershire) uncovered a Celtic grave which once contained three bodies, though only the skull of a woman still survived.

Jewellery, including amber and a silver-gilt brooch of a type usually found in Norfolk or Humberside, were by her side. For a short time this grave raised serious hopes that this might have been the last resting place of Boudica and her daughters, before this theory was disproved.

The Internet reveals yet another side of a burgeoning and seemingly unstoppable legacy, and helps to underline and emphasise the raw power of a name which has now been brought into service to attract and inspire new generations. Internet searches reveal that the name is currently used, for example, for dress shops, a British fashion label, designer shoes on-line, theatre dramas, encyclopaedias, history sites, films and film companies, travel agents, jewellery, beer (including an Iceni brewery), a walking robot, a motor yacht and a cruise liner.

So here, perhaps, is the modern way of putting her attraction to the test. For those of you with Internet access, go to Google and type in her name, using Boudica, Boudicca or Boadicea. The first (accessed February, 2006) produces 279,000 entries; the second a staggering 1,200,000 entries; and the third 327,000 entries.

Today, at long last, archaeology is enabling us to separate the real story of Boudica from the myth. The mythical story has led to her being revered as a larger than life figure. Sometimes it is even forgotten that she was a real person. But she was real, and she did tread the land of northern East Anglia. At long last we know some of the settlements that she must have visited, and know much more about her life, her times and her people. This new understanding also serves to enrich still further the inspirational story that is her legacy. Today, two thousand years on, Boudica, her achievements and her tribe, have never been more venerated or more important.

Beer mats from a modern brewery sited within the territory of the ancient Iceni people

OPPOSITE: *It seems entirely appropriate that the Queen's Head in East Anglia should carry an image of Boudica.*

RIGHT: *A variety of businesses in East Anglia have made use of the name Iceni.*

Archaeologists at work in September
2009 at Caistor St Edmund (which
the Romans knew as Venta Icenorum).
It is this sort of painstaking investiga-
tion that may one day enable us to
understand more of the time of the Iceni.
However, the site is so extensive that
it is likely to be some time before a full
excavation can be undertaken here.

Further Reading

V. Collingridge, *Boudica* (Ebury Press, 2000)

J. Davies, *The Land of Boudica: Prehistoric and Roman Norfolk* (Heritage, 2009)

J. Davies & T. Williamson, *Land of the Iceni: The Iron Age in Northern East Anglia* (Norwich: Centre of East Anglian Studies, 1999)

R. Hingley & C. Unwin, *Boudica: Iron Age Warrior Queen* (Hambledon & London, 2005)

B. Robinson & T. Gregory, *Celtic Fire & Roman Rule*, 2nd edition (Cromer: Poppyland, 2003)

Paul R. Sealey, *The Boudican Revolt Against Rome* (Shire, 1997)

G. Webster, *Boudica: The British Revolt Against Rome* AD 60 (Batsford, 1978)

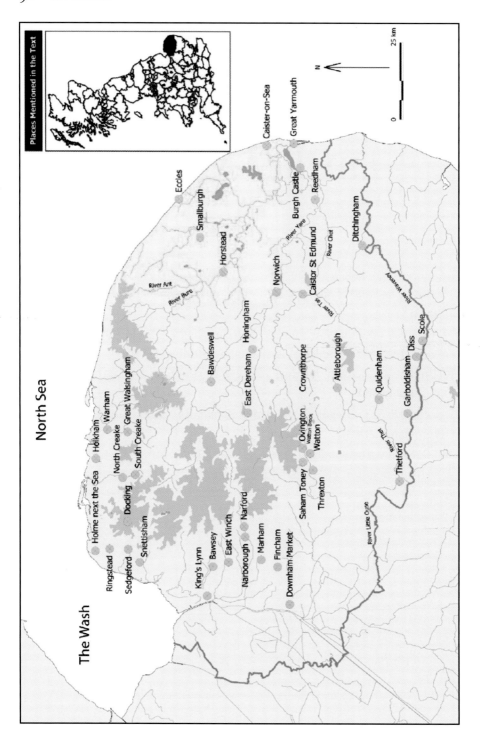

Places to visit

Venta Icenorum Roman town

The site lies three miles south of Norwich in the parish of Caistor St
Edmund. Well-preserved late Roman town walls. The area was once occupied
by Iron Age settlement. There are interpretation panels and a riverside walk.
The site is owned by the Norfolk Archaeological Trust and is open to the
public. Guidebook: J. A. Davies, *Venta Icenorum: Caistor St Edmund Roman
Town* (Norfolk Archaeological Trust, 2001). ISBN 0 9540676 0 6.

South Creake

Located beside the Syderstone Road about 0.6 mile (1 km) south-west
of South Creake village, near Fakenham. The site of a circular Iron Age
earthwork enclosure of hillfort type. The earthworks have now been
flattened. The site is owned by the Norfolk Archaeological Trust and is open
to the public.

Holkham

Located two and a half miles (4 km) west of Wells-next-the-Sea, 0.6 mile
(1 km) from the sea. Set within Holkham Marshes and adjacent to pine

woods. An Iron Age earthwork enclosure of hillfort type, originally built on the south end of a curving sandspit. Possibly the stronghold stormed by the Romans during the rebellion of AD 47. Viewable from a raised bird hide.

Norwich, Castle Museum and Art Gallery

The Boudica Gallery within Norwich Castle tells the story of the revolt against the Romans through the eyes of the Iceni. Many artefacts of the period are displayed, including the magnificent Snettisham Treasure.

Thetford Castle

Situated within the south east of the town in a meander of the River Thet, adjacent to Nuns' Bridges. Earthworks and ditches belonging to an Iron Age enclosure of hillfort type. The earthworks were subsequently remodelled as part of a Norman castle, when a motte (mound) was also added. The site is accessible to the public.

Warham Camp

Situated 2 miles (3 km) south-east of Wells-next-the-Sea, south of Warham village. A double circuit of ramparts and ditches form the most spectacular earthworks in the county. Another Iron Age enclosure of hillfort type. The site is accessible to the public.

Boudica's Way

A designated walk which covers 38 miles (61 km) between Diss and *Venta Icenorum*, passing through the villages of Tasburgh, Saxlingham Green, Shotesham and Upper Stoke.

Index